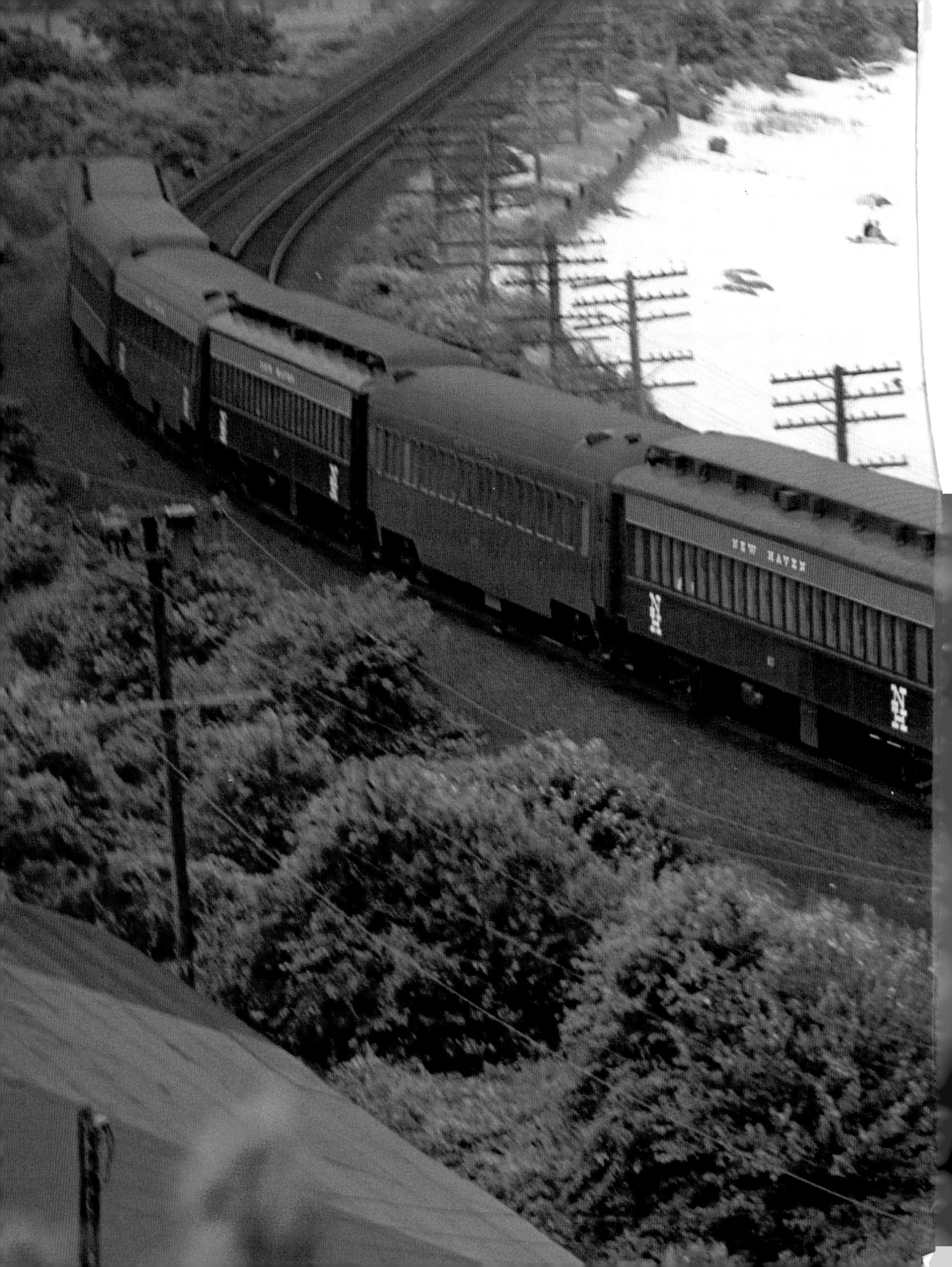
NEW HAVEN

TIMETABLE

Effective March 1, 1949

EASTERN STANDARD TIME

The New York New Haven and Hartford

RAILROAD CO.

**THE SCENIC SHORELINE ROUTE SERVING
NEW YORK AND NEW ENGLAND**

NEW HAVEN
RAILROAD

PETER E. LYNCH

MBI

This edition first published in 2003 by
MBI Publishing Company, Galtier Plaza,
Suite 200, 380 Jackson Street, St. Paul, MN
55101-3885 USA

MBI Publishing Company titles are also
available at discounts in bulk quantity for
industrial or sales-promotional use. For
details write to Special Sales Manager at
Motorbooks International Wholesalers &
Distributors, Galtier Plaza, Suite 200,
380 Jackson Street, St. Paul, MN
55101-3885 USA

Library of Congress Cataloging-in-
Publication Data Available

ISBN 0-7603-1441-1

On the front cover: No. 312, an electric
built in 1923 and one of only two EP-2s
that had the 1956 "McGinnis" paint
scheme, heads west near Southport,
Connecticut, in 1957. The catenary
construction here is the "floating beam"
type used between Stamford and New
Haven. The wires are not directly attached
to a catenary structure, but rather to a pair
of steel beams on each side of the structure.
Thomas J. McNamara

On the frontispiece: 1949 New Haven
Railroad timetable.

On the title page: In the summer of 1957
a westbound passes the beach of Rocky
Neck State Park in Connecticut.
Thomas J. McNamara

On the back cover: *Yankee Clipper* No. 23
heads west near Leetes Island, Connecticut,
with Fairbanks-Morse "C" Liner 793 in
green and gold in 1958. *Thomas J. McNamara*

Edited by Dennis Pernu
Designed by LeAnn Kuhlmann

Printed in China

CONTENTS

DEDICATION

This New Haven Railroad book is dedicated to Thomas J. McNamara, who along with his friend, the late Kent Cochrane, faithfully documented on film the New York, New Haven & Hartford Railroad for its last 25 years. Many have taken extensive photographs of the New Haven but none so comprehensively. Without Tom McNamara's work, this book would not have been possible.

This book is also dedicated to the employees of the New Haven Railroad. More than the locomotives and track, a railroad consists of the people who show up every day and make it run. The employees of the New Haven—the engineers, conductors, trackmen, and yardmasters, among others—are the ones who kept this railroad, which was in turmoil for most of its existence, together.

ACKNOWLEDGMENTS

Several sources of information were particularly helpful in preparing this book. *New Haven Power 1838–1968* by J. W. Swanberg is an essential work for anyone interested in a detailed and complete study of all New Haven locomotives. *The Rail Lines of Southern New England* by Ronald Dale Karr was extremely helpful in tracing the complex history of the 175 predecessor rail lines that formed the New Haven system. This fine work is also essential for anyone interested in the detailed history of every rail line in Connecticut, Rhode Island, and Massachusetts. The corporate archives of the New Haven, located at the University of Connecticut at Storrs, are overwhelmed with New Haven documents, expertly and helpfully managed by Laura Katz Smith.

Beyond the work of Tom McNamara, I am thankful for the help of Peter McLachlan, Arthur E. Mitchell, Richard A. Selva, George E. Ford, Fielding L. Bowman, Al Lawrence, David W. Jacobs, Robert Liljestrand, and Ben Perry, Jr. I thank Jack Swanberg for his manuscript review and for sharing his vast knowledge in supplying valuable information and for making many corrections. I thank my wife, Kathryn, and my daughter, Kelley, for bearing with me as I put in time on this project.

INTRODUCTION

More than three decades since its disappearance into the Penn Central system, the New Haven Railroad—officially the New York, New Haven & Hartford Railroad Company (NYNH&H)—still holds great fascination for many. The intent of this book is to give the reader an insight into the New Haven's role in New England transportation by presenting a brief overview of its history and operations. It was a small railroad in terms of route mileage, operating in three small states—Connecticut, Rhode Island, and Massachusetts—plus a small corner of southeastern New York. At its greatest extent, the New Haven had less than one percent of the nation's total railroad route miles. Yet its total track mileage made it a medium-size railroad for many years.

On this small railroad one could find an example of just about every type of railroading. After the Long Island, the New Haven derived more of its total revenue

EP-3 No. 352 hauls a westbound passenger train from Boston through Riverside, Connecticut, in 1956. *Thomas J. McNamara*

from passenger service than any other railroad in the nation; in fact, in 1924, one of every ten American rail passengers traveled on the New Haven. It ran trains with sleeping cars and Pullman parlor cars, branchline trains, commuter trains, mail and express trains, circus trains, and troop trains. It ran excursion trains to baseball games, football games, the Bronx Zoo, ski slopes, horse races, the New York Flower Show, summer camps, and other attractions. Many commuter trains had bar cars, which, during the depths of the railroad's financial woes, were said to be its only profitable operation. Until the 1930s, the railroad operated overnight steamers from Fall River, Massachusetts, to New York City. It ran passenger ferries to the exclusive resorts of Martha's Vineyard and Nantucket. The New Haven's passenger operations were closely interwoven with the lives of the people along its lines—they used the trains to get to work, school, and entertainment and cultural attractions.

In its freight operations, the New Haven was every bit as diverse, carrying almost every kind of commodity that moved by rail. It had 125-car freight trains and two-car branchline local freights. When opened in 1925, Cedar Hill Yard in New Haven was the largest rail classification yard east of the Mississippi River. The New Haven even had its own navy, with tugs shuttling car floats between its two yards in Brooklyn's Bay Ridge and Oak Point in the Bronx and the New Jersey side of the Hudson River.

The New Haven's strengths and weaknesses were interwoven. Ironically, its initial domination of the region's transportation was a major cause of its downfall. It could not sustain its overexpansion and the resulting debt. But despite its dark financial history, the New Haven was a colorful and innovative member of the nation's rail industry for nearly a century.

Above: On the Friday of Memorial Day weekend 1959, RS-3s 532 and 538 bring train No. 144, the *Berkshire*, north through Brookfield, Connecticut. *Peter McLachlan*

Left: Train No. 138 arrives in Lee, an industrial town in Berkshire County, Massachusetts, in 1968. *George E. Ford*

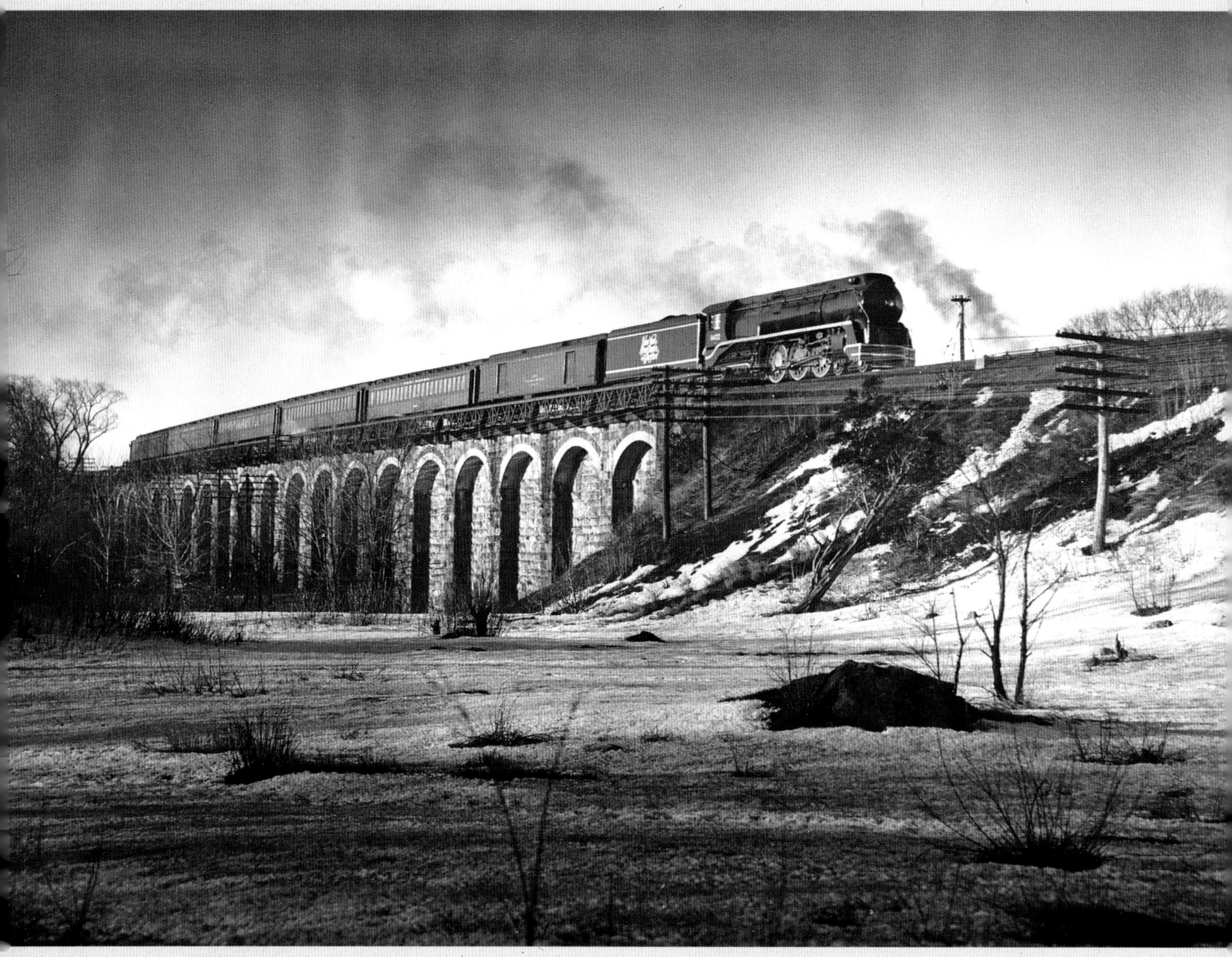

CHAPTER ONE

SETTING THE STAGE

Many Lines Become the New Haven System

Significant rail construction in southern New England began in the early-1830s and proceeded at a rapid rate until the Civil War. As the nineteenth century passed, many small new lines emerged and were consolidated into larger ones. By the 1890s, all had joined one of four systems: the Consolidated, the Old Colony, the New York & England (NY&E), or the Central New England (CNE). Because of the many bankruptcies, failures, takeovers, and mergers that these companies endured as

In 1948 a westbound Boston–Providence local crosses the Canton Viaduct in the structure's 113th year of service. This impressive locomotive was on a local because, just out of Readville Shop for periodic maintenance, a shakedown run to Providence was needed before going back on the Shore Line expresses. *Kent Cochrane. Thomas J. McNamara Collection*

they were forged into the New Haven system, the railroad's history is complex. Though it peaked at 2,256 route miles, it was formed by the consolidation of 175 companies.

The "Consolidated"

In 1872 the Hartford & New Haven (H&NH) merged with the New York & New Haven (NY&NH) to form the New York, New Haven & Hartford Railroad Company, known for many years as the "Consolidated." In 1836 the H&NH began construction of 61 miles of track north from the port in New Haven to Hartford, reaching Springfield, Massachusetts, by 1844. Branches in Connecticut from Berlin to New Britain and from Windsor Locks to Suffield were also built. Connecting west from New Haven were 60 miles of track to Woodlawn in the Bronx built by the NY&NH between 1847 and 1849.

In 1848 the NY&NH reached agreement with the New York & Harlem (NY&H) and

the New York Central (NYC) Railroads to operate over the 13 miles from Woodlawn into New York City, where 27th Street Station in Manhattan was used until 1872. The station was then relocated to Grand Central Depot on 42nd Street in 1899 and renamed Grand Central Station. It finally became Grand Central Terminal when reconstructed in 1913.

By 1854 the entire NY&NH was double-track, and the four-tracking began in 1884. In 1868, the 8-mile New Canaan Branch from Stamford was built in Connecticut, and the NY&NH took over the 12-mile Harlem River & Port Chester Railroad from New Rochelle, New York, to the north bank of the Harlem River in the Bronx, providing freight and passenger access west and south via car-float across the Hudson River to New Jersey.

The Consolidated was the parent and the heart of what became the New Haven Railroad. Although the Consolidated initially controlled the track that ran east from New

1954 New Haven Railroad system map.

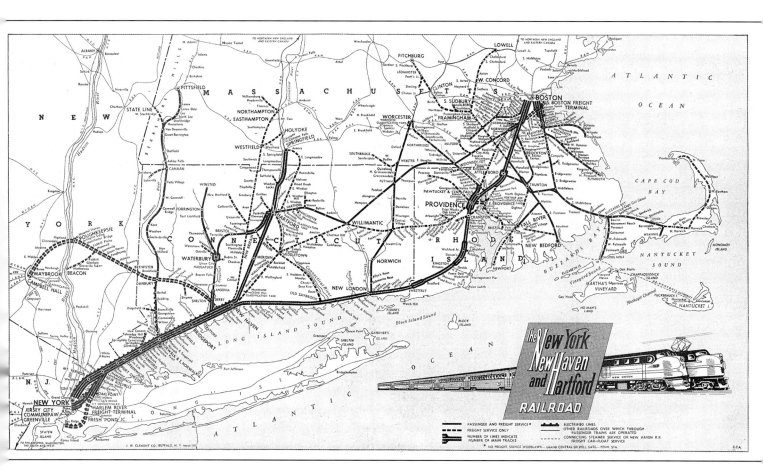

York to New Haven, Connecticut, and then north through Hartford to Springfield, Massachusetts, it proceeded to take over nearly every connecting line in Connecticut, Rhode Island, and Massachusetts. A key acquisition for the Consolidated was the Shore Line route from New Haven to Providence. Between 1832 and 1837 the New York, Providence & Boston (NYP&B) built 44 miles of track from Providence to Stonington, Connecticut, where steamboat service was offered via Long Island Sound to New York City. In the 1850s the New Haven & New London (NH&NL) constructed 50 miles of track along the coast of Long Island Sound from New Haven to the west bank of the Thames River in New London. In 1858 the NYP&B completed a 12-mile extension west from Stonington to the east bank of the Thames in Groton, and, the same year, took control of the NH&NL. However, because

the trip between New York and Providence required changing trains at New Haven, as well as ferry crossings at Saybrook and New London, the union did not prove feasible and ended in 1862.

In 1870, once the NH&NL had completed its bridge across the Connecticut River at Saybrook, the New York & New Haven took it over. The Consolidated then waited until 1892 to take over the NYP&B, three years after that road completed an expensive bridge across the Thames River between New London and Groton. This provided an all-rail route from New York City to Providence where a connection could be made to Boston. Included in the NYP&B was the Providence & Worcester Railroad, which had built 43 miles of track between these two cities in 1847. In anticipation of the takeover of the NYP&B, the Consolidated absorbed the Providence, Warren & Bristol, a 24-mile line

In 1948 a westbound New Haven train to Grand Central enters the New York Central Harlem Division at Woodlawn, operating under the trackage agreement in effect for a century. The pantographs on the locomotive were not raised and the train was operating on DC third-rail power. *Kent Cochrane. Thomas J. McNamara Collection*

built in the 1850s that crossed the Seekonk River from Providence to East Providence and ran along the east side of Narragansett Bay south to Warren and Bristol, Rhode Island, with a branch to Fall River, Massachusetts.

In the 1880s the Consolidated acquired four north–south connecting lines. The first, in 1882, was the Air Line Railroad, with 54 miles between New Haven, Middletown, and Willimantic, Connecticut. Finished in 1873, it was to be a short route to Boston. Its significant grades, two long viaducts, and generally remote trackage prevented it from succeeding on its own. Five years later, in 1887, the other three lines were acquired. The Naugatuck ("Naugy"), entirely in Connecticut and completed in 1849, ran north for 55 miles from Devon, just east of Bridgeport, through heavily industrialized Derby, Waterbury, and Torrington before terminating in Winsted. The New Haven & Northampton (NH&N), built between 1847 and 1871, ran 87 miles from New Haven to Westfield and Northampton, Massachusetts, with a 9-mile branch from

Westfield to Holyoke. Some of this line became known as the "Canal" because it was built, in part, on the right-of-way of an abandoned canal. The Connecticut Valley line was built during the 1860s and extended 46 miles from Hartford south through Middletown to Saybrook Point. It paralleled the Connecticut River and was lightly used except in the summer months, when it transported people from Hartford to the shore of Long Island Sound in the Saybrook area.

In 1892 the Housatonic Railroad, which connected with the Consolidated in three Connecticut locations—South Norwalk, Bridgeport, and Derby—was acquired. Its 157 miles became two significant New Haven lines. The first was the Berkshire Line, which ran north from South Norwalk through Danbury and New Milford in Connecticut to Pittsfield, Massachusetts, with a 10-mile freight branch to the Massachusetts-New York state line to make a connection with the Boston & Albany Railroad (B&A). The second was the Connecticut portion of the Maybrook freight line between Danbury and

Derby Junction. The Housatonic, named for the river it paralleled, originally built track north from Bridgeport, Connecticut, in 1837 reaching Pittsfield in 1850. Included in the Housatonic was the Danbury & Norwalk (D&N), built in the 1850s with 24 miles between these two Connecticut cities. This line was important for the Housatonic to get a shorter and faster route to New York via Norwalk instead of Bridgeport. In 1886 the Housatonic had taken over the D&N and in 1888 added 10 miles of track from Newtown, Connecticut, to Derby Junction to connect to the Consolidated.

Old Colony

A dozen small railroads formed the Old Colony system in the Boston area. First constructed and most important was the 44-mile Boston & Providence (B&P) completed between those two state capitals in 1835. Carefully engineered to have mostly straight track, the B&P had a 70-foot-high, 615-foot-long stone-arch, double-track viaduct over a valley formed by the Neponset River between Canton and Sharon, Massachusetts. Originally, the B&P terminated in East Providence, requiring a ferry connection into Providence for passengers wanting to take the NYP&B to New York. In 1847 the B&P built a new line from Attleboro, Massachusetts, to Pawtucket, Rhode Island, where the B&P shared trackage with the Providence & Worcester into downtown Providence. Foresight in construction of the Canton Viaduct allowed the entire B&P

This bridge, built in 1919, replaced the original 1889 bridge over the Thames River between Groton and New London that was the last link in the Shore Line route. In 1948, an eastbound New York–Boston passenger train is met by a westbound freight. *Kent Cochrane. Thomas J. McNamara Collection*

15

Above: The 1875 Park Square Station, located near the current Back Bay Station in Boston, belonged first to the Boston & Providence and then to the Old Colony. It was replaced by South Station in 1899. *Bob Liljestrand Collection*

Right: The Poughkeepsie Bridge, completed in 1888 across the Hudson River, was the reason the Consolidated acquired the Central New England Railway: to provide a connection to the west. The bridge and its approaches were 6,768 feet long and 212 feet above the river. The bridge originally had two tracks, which were overlapped in a gauntlet in 1917 to accommodate heavier steam power, like that shown here in 1947. *Kent Cochrane. Thomas J. McNamara Collection*

to be double-tracked in 1860. Its mainline, along with its Stoughton and Dedham Branches, allowed the B&P to connect Boston with many southeastern Massachusetts communities as well as Providence. In 1875, to serve this growing traffic in Boston, an elaborate depot on Park Square, not far from the current Back Bay Station, was built. In 1888 the B&P joined the Old Colony system.

The original Old Colony Railroad was built south from Boston to Braintree and then southeast to Plymouth in 1846, a distance of 37 miles. Its access to Boston gave it a much stronger position than the other lines in southeastern Massachusetts, so that in 1872 it took over four lines, constructed between 1844 and 1864: the Fall River Railroad, the Dighton & Somerset, the Newport & Fall River, and the Cape Cod. This consolidation

gave the Old Colony more than 200 route miles from Boston and Braintree south to Cape Cod and Fall River. The Woods Hole Branch, built in the 1870s, shortened the ferry trip to the popular resort islands of Martha's Vineyard and Nantucket. In 1877 the Old Colony took over its fifth line, the South Shore, extending 37 miles to Greenbush and Kingston, where it connected with the Old Colony Plymouth Line.

Similar to the Consolidated, the Old Colony absorbed other lines, including the 142-mile Boston, Clinton, Fitchburg & New Bedford in 1879. This line was formed between 1872 and 1876 by the union of five

Massachusetts railroads: the New Bedford & Taunton, the Fitchburg & Worcester, the Agricultural Branch, the Framingham & Lowell, and the Mansfield & Framingham. These lines, built between 1848 and 1871, ran north from coastal New Bedford via Mansfield to Framingham, then northwest to Fitchburg and north to Lowell, with a branch from Taunton to Attleboro to connect with the Boston & Providence.

By 1890 the Old Colony connected Boston with Providence and every significant community located in southeastern Massachusetts. There were so many lines that some towns had multiple routes to Boston.

The Old Colony consolidation also provided inland freight access from the ports at New Bedford and Fall River to Boston and Maine lines at Lowell and Fitchburg, and to the Boston & Albany at Framingham.

The New York & New England

The Boston, Hartford & Erie Railroad (BH&E) was established in 1863 to form a rail system from Boston west by consolidating and extending existing lines. Between the end of the Civil War and 1869, the BH&E took over five lines: the Norfolk County, the Midland, the Southbridge & Blackstone, the Charles River, and the Norwich & Worcester.

The New Britain, Connecticut, station along the New York & New England line between Waterbury and Boston was built in 1886. It also served Consolidated trains from Berlin, where they connected with Hartford line trains to New York.

The New Haven Railroad boasted numerous dedicated employees with long service. Elmer S. Meyerhoff started with the New Haven in 1886 and retired in 1956, with service spanning almost the entire life of the New Haven. He is seen here working as a tower operator at signal station 38 in Stamford.

The BH&E timed its takeover of the Southbridge & Blackstone to occur in 1869, the same year that road completed a 20-year effort to build 49 miles from Blackstone to Willimantic. The BH&E then had nearly 200 route miles west from Boston via Dorchester through Walpole and Blackstone, Massachusetts, and on to Putnam and Willimantic, in Connecticut (later known on the New Haven as the Midland Division), with another route from Boston through Needham and to Woonsocket, Rhode Island. At Putnam, the east-west line connected to the north-south Norwich & Worcester from Worcester, Massachusetts, through Plainfield and Norwich to Allyns Point, Connecticut, where a passenger could catch a boat to New York City. The Boston, Hartford & Erie became the New York & New England Railroad (NY&NE) in 1873.

In the early nineteenth century, railroads generally followed the coastline or inland rivers so that grades and other obstacles were not severe. In the late-1840s construction began on an inland line known as the Hartford, Providence & Fishkill (HP&F).

The intent of this road was to establish a connection with western carriers by floating railcars on barges across the Hudson River at Fishkill Landing (renamed Beacon in 1914), about 50 miles north of New York City. Inland Connecticut, however, presented numerous difficulties in the construction of east-west rail lines. Parts of the state are very hilly and heavily wooded, dotted with many small lakes, and crisscrossed by meandering streams, which added greatly to the HP&F's construction time and cost. The 90 rail miles between Providence and Hartford alone were 50 percent greater than the straight-line distance. Other obstacles were perpendicular rail lines of competing companies in their path and farmers' fields, which competitors routinely bought to obstruct and delay new construction. By 1855 the HP&F had constructed 121 miles from Providence to Waterbury, Connecticut, via Willimantic, Hartford, New Britain, and Bristol, Connecticut. Two years later it was bankrupt but continued to operate. In 1878 this line was taken over by the NY&NE, to which it connected in Willimantic.

In 1880 the NY&NE was extended 30 miles from Waterbury to Danbury. The next year the line crossed over into New York state when 34 more miles were built west to Hopewell Junction, connecting to the Newburgh, Dutchess & Connecticut's 11.6-mile line to Wicopee Junction, from which the NY&NE constructed a line of a mile and a half to Fishkill Landing. This gave the NY&NE a route from Boston to western connections without the need to deal with the Consolidated. The NY&NE and the Consolidated did however cooperate to run the first through-passenger trains between New York and Boston. Trains ran between New York, New Haven, and Hartford on the Consolidated and then on the NY&NE via Willimantic and Putnam, to Boston. The premier train, *The New England Limited*, took six hours on this route in the 1880s. It was rerouted via the Air Line through Middletown in 1891 with new equipment painted white and trimmed with

gold. It was officially known as the *White Train* and, familiarly, as the *Ghost Train*.

Central New England

In 1869 the Connecticut Western began constructing track west from Hartford toward Poughkeepsie, New York. Through the 1870s, this road faced problems similar to those encountered by the HP&F. It wound a tortured route over grades that prevented it from being a heavy tonnage route. In Connecticut and New York, it ran through remote areas with little freight business and few significant towns without an established railroad. By 1880 it was bankrupt and it reorganized as the Hartford & Connecticut Western (H&CW). It was later taken over by the Central New England & Western (CNE&W), a company that extended east from Campbell Hall and Maybrook, New York, and had recently completed the bridge across the Hudson River between Poughkeepsie and Highland, New York, in 1888. Four years later the CNE&W—allied with the Reading Railroad and its coal interests in Eastern Pennsylvania—was reorganized into the Philadelphia, Reading & New England (PR&NE). This road was eager to move coal and other goods into New

In 1965, the *Yankee Clipper* No. 22 races east through Kingston, Rhode Island, toward Boston. This station, built by the New York, Providence & Boston in 1875, continues to serve Amtrak passengers bound for the University of Rhode Island, Newport, and other shore points in the twenty-first century. *David W. Jacobs*

19

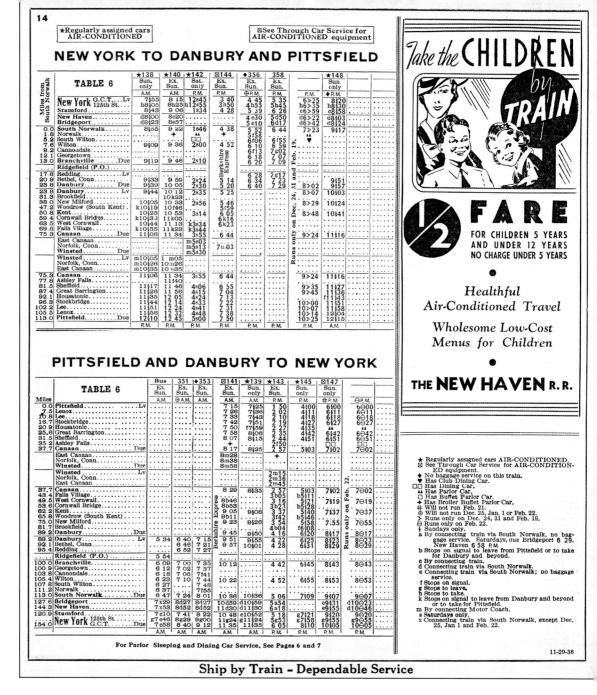

New Haven Railroad timetable dated November 29, 1936.

England on its all-rail route, in competition with the Consolidated, which had to move railcars across New York harbor by barge. The PR&NE tried and failed to seize control of the New York & New England in the mid-1890s. It was reorganized as the Central New England Railway in 1899 with just over 200 miles of track from Hartford west through Canaan, Connecticut, and to Hopewell Junction, Poughkeepsie, and Maybrook, New York.

The New Haven Comes Together

In 1892 J. Pierpont Morgan joined the New Haven board of directors, formalizing a long association between his family and the New Haven Railroad. An original investor in the Hartford & New Haven had been Hartford resident Joseph Morgan, grandfather of J.P. In 1893, the year after the Consolidated reached Providence, it arranged a long-term lease of the Old Colony system, giving the New Haven control of the Shore Line route from New York to Boston and all rail lines in eastern Massachusetts south of Boston. Between 1895 and 1898 the New Haven took control, then ownership, of the NY&NE, ending that road's long struggle to remain independent and giving the New Haven an inland route

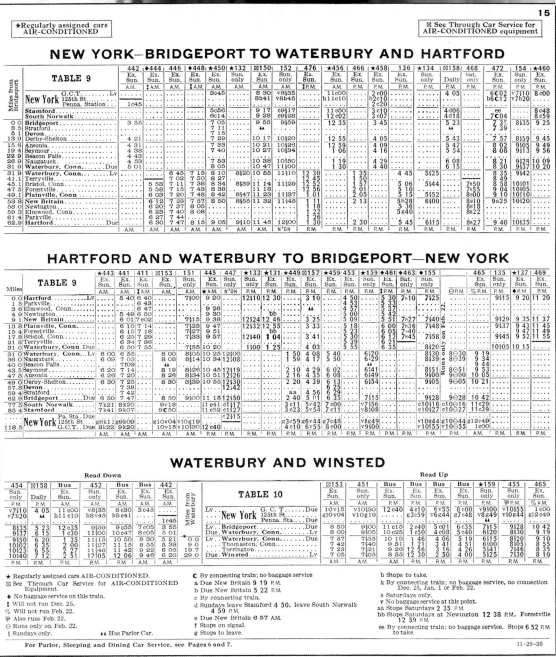

NEW YORK—BRIDGEPORT TO WATERBURY AND HARTFORD

TABLE 9	442 Ex. Sun.	◆444 Ex. Sun.	446 Ex. Sun.	◆448 Ex. Sun.	★450 Ex. Sun.	★132 Sun. only	⊠150 Ex. Sun.	152 Sun. only	476 Ex. Sun.	★456 Ex. Sun.	466 Ex. Sun.	★458 Ex. Sun.	136 Sun. only	★134 Daily	⊠158 Sat. only	468 Ex. Sun.	472 Ex. Sun.	154 Sun. only	★460 Ex. Sun.
New York G.C.T. Lv					3c45		8 30	v8↓35		11c00		2c00				4 05	6C02	v7↓10	8 00
125th St.							8h41	v8h45		h11c10		h2c10					h6C12	v7h20	
Penna. Station .. Lv		1c45										2c20							
Stamford					5c56		9 17	c9↓17		11 c50		3 c10				4 06			8 48
South Norwalk ..					6c14		9 28	c9↓28		12 c02		3 c07				4 18	7C04		8 59
0 0 Bridgeport......	3 55				7 05		9 55	9↓59		12 35		3 45				5 23	7 ↓5	8↓35	9 25
3 5 Stratford........					7 11												7 39		
5 1 Devon..........					7 15														
13 9 Derby-Shelton..	4 21				7 29		10 17	10↓20		12 55		4 05				5 43	7 57	8↓59	9 45
15 6 Ansonia........	4 31				7 33		10 21	10↓26		12 59		4 09				5 47	8 02	9↓05	9 49
19 4 Seymour........	4 38				7 40		10 27	10↓34		1 06		4 16				5 54	8 08	9↓13	9 56
22 9 Beacon Falls...	4 43				7 53		10 38	10↓50								6 08	8 21	9↓28	10 09
26 9 Naugatuck.....	4 53						10 42	10↓53		1 19		4 29							
31 9 Waterbury, Conn...Due	5 01				8 05		10 47	11↓00		1 30		4 40				6 15	8 30	9↓37	10 20
31 9 Waterbury, Conn...Lv			6 45	7 15	8 10	8↓20	10 55	11↓10	12 30		1 35		4 45	5↓25			8 35	9↓42	
41 1 Terryville......			7 02	7 30	8 27				12 45		1 50						8 49		
45 1 Bristol, Conn..		5 53	7 11	7 38	8 34	8↓39	11 14	11↓29	12 52		1 57		5 06	5↓44		7↓50	8 55	10↓01	
47 5 Forestville.....		5 58	7 15	7 43	8 38		11 18		12 56		2 01					7↓55	9 04	10↓05	
49 1 Plainville, Conn.		6 03	7 20	7 48	8 42	8↓47	11 23	11↓37	1 01		2 05		5 15	5↓52		8↓00	9 10	10↓10	
53 8 New Britain		6 12	7 29	7 57	8 50	8↓55	11 32	11↓45	1 11		2 13		5h28	6↓00		8↓10	9a25	10↓20	
58 0 Newington......		6 20	7 37	8 05					1 18				5 36			8↓18			
59 3 Elmwood, Conn.		6 23	7 40	8 08					1 22				5↓40			8↓22			
61 4 Parkville........		6 27	7 44						1 26										
62 9 Hartford.......Due		6 30	7 47	8 15	9 05	9↓10	11 45	12↓00	1 30		2 30		5 45	6↓15		8↓27	9 40	10↓35	
	A.M.	A.M.	A.M.	A.M.	A.M.	A.M.	A.M.	N'ON	P.M.	P.M.	P.M.	P.M.	P.M.	P.M.	P.M.	P.M.	P.M.	P.M.	P.M.

HARTFORD AND WATERBURY TO BRIDGEPORT—NEW YORK

TABLE 9	★443 Ex. Sun.	441 Ex. Sun.	411 Ex. Sun.	⊠153 Ex. Sun.	151 Sun. only	445 Ex. Sun.	447 Sun. only	★133 Sun. only	★131 Ex. Sun.	★449 Ex. Sun.	⊠157 Ex. Sun.	★459 Ex. Sun.	453 Ex. Sun.	★159 Sun. only	◆461 Ex. Sun.	◆463 Sat. only	★155 Ex. Sun.	465 Ex. Sun.	135 Sun. only	★137 Ex. Sun.	469 Ex. Sun.
0 0 Hartford......Lv	5 40	6 40		7↓00	9 20		12↓10	12 30		3 10		4 50		5 30	7↓10	7↓25			9↓15	9 20	11 20
1 5 Parkville........		6 43			9 26							4 53		5 33							
3 6 Elmwood, Conn.		6 47			9 30							4 56		5 37							
4 9 Newington......	5 49	6 50			9 30				bb			5 00		5 42							
9 1 New Britain	6 01	7 02		7↓15	9 38		12↓24	12 46		3 25		5 09		5 51	7↓27	7↓40		9↓29	9 35	11 37
13 8 Plainville, Conn.	6 10	7 14		7↓28	9 47		12↓32	12 55		3 33		5 18		6 00	7↓36	7↓48		9↓37	9 43	11 45
15 4 Forestville.....	6 15	7 18		7↓27	9 51			bb				5 23		6 05	7↓40				9 47	11 49
17 8 Bristol, Conn...	6 25	7 29		7↓33	9 57		12↓40	1 04		3 41		5 28		6 17	7↓45	7↓58		9↓45	9 52	11 55
21 8 Terryville......	6 34	7 36										5 34		6 27						
31 0 Waterbury, Conn.Due	6 50	7 55		7↓55	10 20		1↓00	1 25		4 03		5 55		6 35	8↓20			10↓05	10 15	
31 0 Waterbury, Conn..Lv	6 00	6 55		8 00	8↓05	10 25	12↓00		1 50	6 20					8↓30	8↓30		9 19		
36 0 Naugatuck.....	6 09	7 03		8 08	8↓14	10 34	12↓08		1 59	4 17	5 50		6↓29		8↓39	8~28		9 34		
40 0 Beacon Falls...		7↓09																9 44		
43 5 Seymour........	6 20	7 14		8 19	8↓26	10 45	12↓19		2 10	4 29	6 02		6↓41		8↓51	9↓00		9 53		
47 3 Ansonia........	6 26	7 20		8 26	8↓34	10 51	12↓26		2 16	4 35	6 08		6↓49		9↓00	9↓00		10 05		
49 0 Derby-Shelton..	6 30	7 25		8 30	8↓39	10 55	12↓30		2 20	4 39	6 13		6↓54		9↓05	9↓05		10 21		
57 8 Devon..........		7 38					12↓42				6 25									
59 4 Stratford.......		7 42							aa		6 29									
62 9 Bridgeport....Due	6 50	7 47		8 50	9↓00	11 15	12↓50		2 40	5 11	6 35		7↓15		9↓28	9↓28		10 42		
77 5 South Norwalk..	7k21	8k20		9v18		11 c41	c1↓17		3 c11	5v42	7 c00		v7↓56		c10↓16	c10↓16		11↓29		
85 4 Stamford......	7k41	9k07		9C50		11 c52	c1↓52		3 c23	5v54	7 c11		v8↓08		c10↓27	c10↓27		11↓39		
New York Pa. Sta..Due									c 2↓15			g3c59	g6v44	g7c48	v9↓00		10↓44	g10↓44	g12c49	
118.5 125th St..Due	g8k11	g9k09		g10v04	v10g19									4 c10	6v55	8 c00	v9↓00	v10↓55	1 c00	
G.C.T..Due	8k22	9k20		10v15	v10g30	12↓40						g3c59	g6v44	g7c48	v9↓00		10↓55	10↓55	1c00	
	A.M.	A.M.	A.M.	A.M.	A.M.	A.M.	P.M.	P.M.	P.M.	P.M.	P.M.	P.M.	P.M.	P.M.	P.M.	P.M.	A.M.	P.M.	P.M.	P.M.

WATERBURY AND WINSTED

Read Down   **Read Up**

454 Sun. only	⊠158 Daily	Bus Ex. Sun.	452 Sun. only	Bus Ex. Sun.	Bus Sun. only	442 Ex. Sun.	Miles from Waterbury	TABLE 10	⊠153 Ex. Sun.	451 Sun. only	Bus Ex. Sun.	Bus Ex. Sun.	Bus Sun. only	★159 Sun. only	455 Sun. only	465 Ex. Sun.
v7↓10	4 05	11 c00	v8↓35	8c30	3c45			Lv..New York G.C.T...Due	10v15	v10↓30	12 c40	4c10	6v55	8 c00	v10↓55	1 c00
v7h20	▲▲	h11 c10	v8h45	h8c41				125th St.	g10v04	v10g19		g3c59	v6g44	g7c48	v8↓49	v10↓44	g12c49
						1c45		Penna. Sta...Due								
8↓35	5 23	12 c35	9↓59	9c55	7c05	3 55		Lv..Bridgeport......Due	8 50	9↓00	11 c15	2↓40	5 c01	6 35	7↓15	9↓28
9↓37	6 15	1 c30	11↓00	10c47	8c05	5 01		Due..Waterbury, Conn..Lv	8 00	8↓05	1 c50	4 c08	5↓40	6↓20	8↓30	10 42
9↓50	6 20	1 35	11↓15	10 50	8 30	5 30	0 0	Lv..Waterbury, Conn...Due	7 57	7↓55	10 19	1 46	4 06	5 19	6↓15	8↓20
10↓02	6 35	2 00	11↓27	11 16	8 55	5 38		..Thomaston, Conn...	7 42	7↓40	9 51	1 21	3 41	4 51	6↓00	8↓05
10↓23	6 55	2 27	11↓48	11 42	9 22	6 05	19.7	..Torrington........	7 23	7↓21	9 26	12 56	3 16	4 26	5↓41	7↓46
10↓40	7 12	2 51	12↓05	12 06	9 46	6 20	29.0	Due..Winsted........Lv	7 05	7↓05	8 55	12 30	2 50	4 00	5↓25	7↓30
P.M.	P.M.	P.M.	P.M.	A.M.	A.M.	A.M.			A.M.	A.M.	A.M.	P.M.	P.M.	P.M.	P.M.	P.M.

Travel by Train - in Comfort

from Boston through Hartford to the Hudson River. By this time the Central New England was also financially distressed. It was taken over by the New Haven in 1904, completing the consolidation of the many rail lines that became the New Haven system.

In 1904 an effort to expand west was thwarted when an attempt by the New Haven to control the Lehigh & Hudson River Railroad (L&HR) failed. The L&HR, extending from Maybrook to Phillipsburg, New Jersey, had direct connections to the Central Railroad of New Jersey (CNJ), the Lackawanna, the Lehigh Valley, and the Central of Pennsylvania. The New Haven sought a direct connection with these lines to get anthracite coal rates that were competitive with those of the Pennsylvania Railroad (PRR) via the New York Harbor floats. Since the New Haven takeover of the L&HR was prevented, the New Haven obtained control of the New York, Ontario & Western. The O&W, as it was known, connected to the New Haven at Maybrook and extended to Oswego on Lake Ontario with a branchline into Carbondale and Scranton in the anthracite area of Pennsylvania. Control of this marginal property served the New Haven's purpose of keeping coal rates in check.

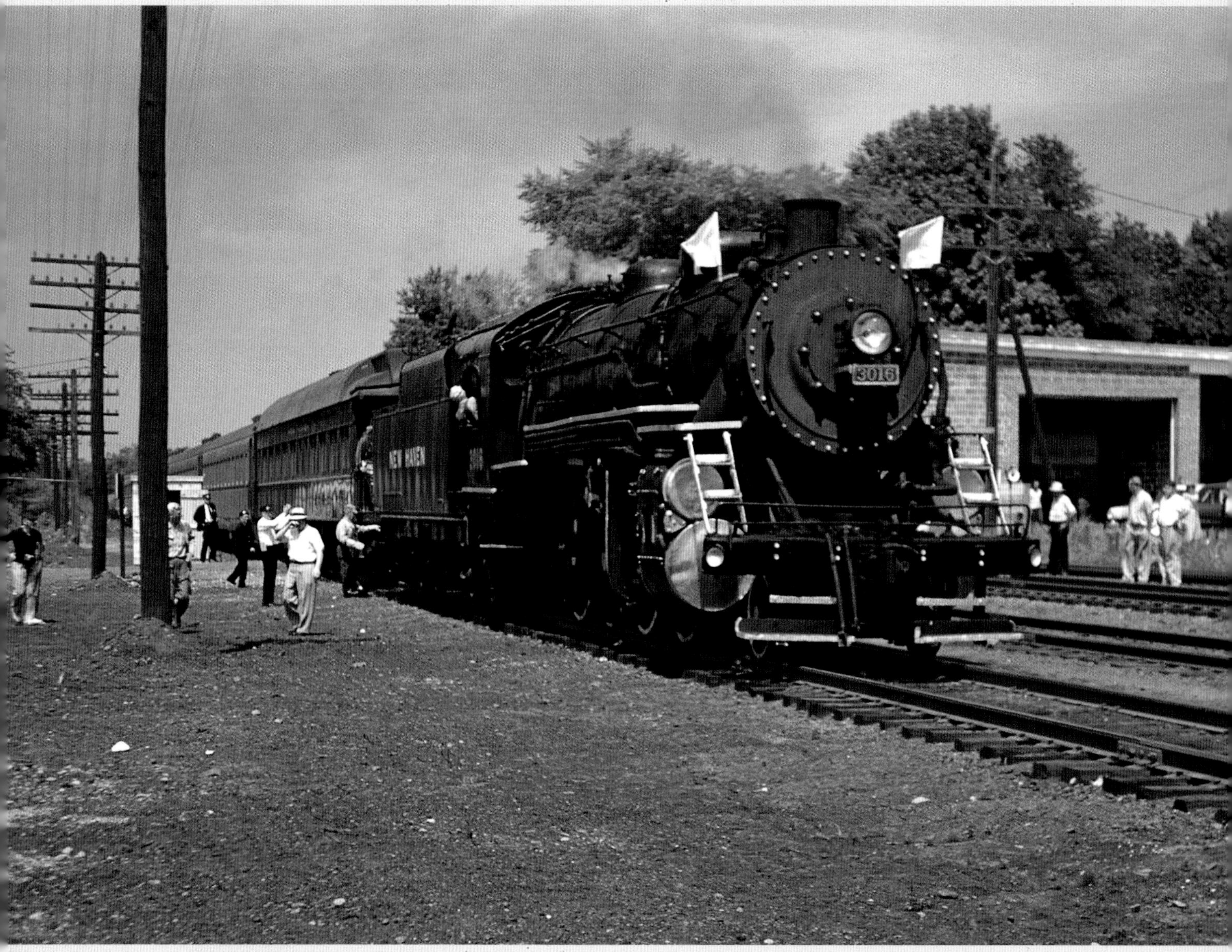
3016
NEW HAVEN

CHAPTER TWO

TRANSFORMATION AND INNOVATION

The 1890s to World War I

Forging the many New Haven lines into a workable, unified rail system between the late-1890s and World War I makes one of the most interesting chapters in New Haven history. This transformation, however, was clouded by the unsatisfied acquisitive tastes of J. Pierpont Morgan. Ron Chernow in his 1990 book, *The House of Morgan,* very succinctly describes the problems brought on by trying to develop the railroad and simultaneously expand in many directions:

Mikados were the first group of heavy tonnage steam locomotives that the New Haven purchased. These 1918 J-Class 2-8-2s had 50 percent more tractive effort than the Moguls and were needed for the heavy tonnage on the Maybrook Line. In 1952 the 3016, one of the few steamers left, was on an excursion through Putnam, Connecticut. *Thomas J. McNamara*

Going on the road's board after 1892, Pierpont came to rule it with a mixture of sentimentality, explosive rage and willful blindness without equal in Morgan annals. In 1903, he had brought in Charles S. Mellen.... The two planned to take over every form of transportation in New England and wantonly usurped steamship lines, interurban electric trolleys, rapid transit system—anything that threatened their monopoly.... The New Haven's expansion was both unwise and unscrupulous. The exorbitant prices paid to swallow up competitors made its debt load crushing. The railroad became a bloated monster of a holding company, with 125,000 employees in 336 subsidiaries.

This expansion was fueled by Morgan's unbounded optimism. He believed that overpayment for any company would soon be justified by the huge economic expansion he had witnessed since the end of the Civil War. But funds needed to improve the railroad and pay the resulting debt were used to purchase money-losing rail and non-rail operations at inflated prices. An example was the Central New England Railroad, acquired in 1904. To obtain 43 miles of track from Hopewell Junction through Poughkeepsie to the western gateways in Maybrook, New York, the New Haven purchased more than 200 miles of Central New England track.

It was not long before all of this began to unravel. The results of the parallel efforts to develop the New Haven system and simultaneously expand in many different directions would plague the New Haven for its entire existence. By 1907 the New Haven, not content to stay in southern New England,

In 1890 and 1891 the Consolidated was expanding the right-of-way to four tracks between South Norwalk and Bridgeport, Connecticut, with construction ongoing in several locations simultaneously. This work site was in East Norwalk.

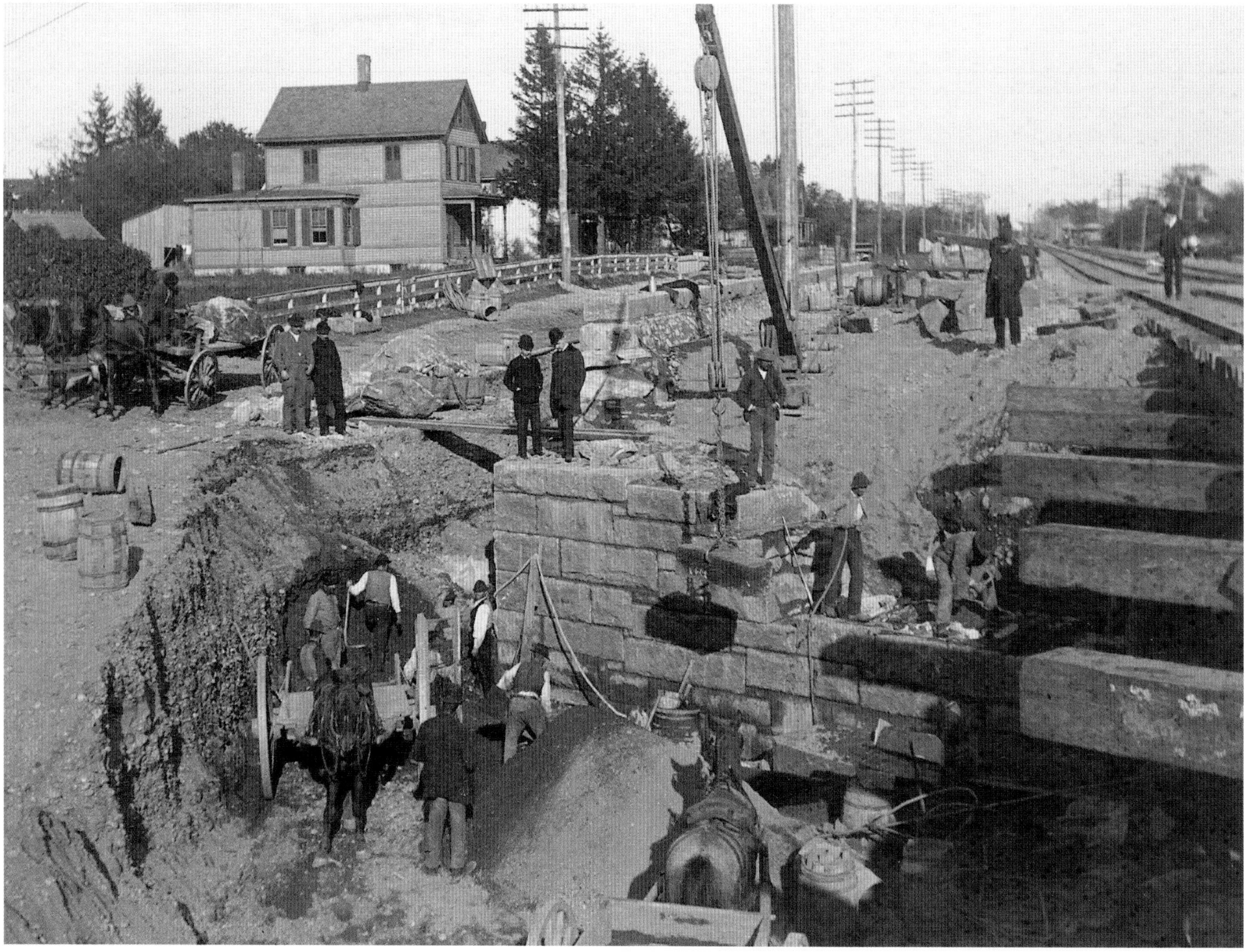

decided to move north and take over the Boston & Maine Railroad (B&M). This endeavor provoked great outcry and resulted in an investigation by the well-known Boston lawyer and eventual Supreme Court Justice Lewis D. Brandeis. The probe and resulting Congressional investigations revealed illegal and shoddy financial practices on the railroad, as well as in other Morgan enterprises. Of course, the New Haven was not Morgan's sole interest. He was simultaneously working to put together the Northern Pacific and Great Northern Railroads, assemble U.S. Steel, consolidate trans-Atlantic merchant shipping, oversee the merger of companies that would become General Electric, dabble in several other trusts, and add to his immense art collection. Brandeis revealed that despite its blue-chip image, the finances of the New

Haven were in poor condition, especially due to non-rail overexpansion. In the midst of continuous bad publicity, the New Haven situation was further aggravated by a number of disastrous train wrecks that killed or injured many passengers during 1911, 1912, and 1913. When Morgan died in 1913, the New Haven changed dramatically. The board of directors was almost completely turned over and Mellen was removed, frequently saying that if Morgan were still alive, he would know what to do.

While this furor prevented the Boston & Maine takeover (the government required that the New Haven divest itself of the B&M stock by 1917), the financial burden remained. The complexity of this problem is well-described in *The New Haven Railroad: Its Rise and Fall* by John L. Weller:

An electric multiple-unit train approaches the station at New Rochelle, New York, heading for Grand Central, 30 minutes away. The cars in this 1954 photo had been in operation for about 40 years. *Thomas J. McNamara*

In Pelham Manor, just west of New Rochelle, the *Senator*, powered by a dual-service EF-3, heads toward Penn Station in 1949. The branch has four tracks, but the catenary structures had room for two more tracks that were removed in the 1930s. *Kent Cochrane. Thomas J. McNamara collection*

Untangling the complicated inter-corporate relationships…required nearly twelve years and was the subject of eleven Interstate Commerce Commission reports, fourteen circuit court decisions and eight decisions of the Supreme Court…. There were thirty-nine intervening groups of security holders, each with lawyers and professional consultants, for whom it was a wonderful and profitable time.

With all of these problems, the New Haven still devoted monumental resources to its plant. In the 1890s the Consolidated was a morass of branchlines running all over three states.

Massive infrastructure work was needed to provide increased capacity. Concentration was focused on the New York–Boston "Shore Line Route." The four-tracking of the line between New York and New Haven, started in 1884, was completed by 1897, with the exception of the area through Bridgeport, which was finished in 1904. Every highway grade crossing was eliminated. Several new stations were built to accommodate the raised and widened right-of-way. A large, new freightyard in East Bridgeport was completed in 1902. Five new four-track drawbridges were constructed across navigable rivers. An automatic signal system on the entire line was completed in 1918.

To comply with smoke prohibitions in downtown Manhattan, in 1907 the first high-voltage AC mainline railroad electrification in the United States was completed on the 22 miles of the Shore Line Route between Woodlawn (its junction with the New York Central) and Stamford, Connecticut. This electrification consisted of an 11,000-volt AC catenary system with wires suspended from elaborate steel lattice structures. Previously electrified at 500 volts DC in 1898 was the single-track Stamford-New Canaan Branch, where a two-car shuttle train connected with trains to and from New York. In 1913 and 1914 the electrification was extended 44 miles east from Stamford through New Haven Station to Cedar Hill Yard. To provide electric power, the New Haven built its own coal-fired powerplant, the first one in America dedicated to strictly rail use, in Cos Cob, Connecticut. This plant, located on the western bank of the Mianus River, could receive coal by rail or barge.

Almost as soon as it began, some of the New Haven's commuter business to New York City was unprofitable because of the per-passenger trackage fee due the New York Central. While the New Haven was completing the first portion of its electrification, Mellen decided to invest in a competing

Opened in 1917, Hell Gate Bridge, with four main tracks across the East River from the South Bronx into Queens, was the New Haven's route to move passengers, mail, express, and freight south and west of New York. *Thomas J. McNamara*

Little Hell Gate on the east approach shows the substantial construction required to reach the main span. The "Shuttle," which ran from Bay Ridge Yard in Brooklyn to Oak Point in the South Bronx, approaches Oak Point, hauled by pre-World War I freight motors in 1953. *Fielding L. Bowman*

company, the New York, Westchester & Boston Railway, on which construction started in 1909. The rationale for the "Westchester," as it was familiarly known, was to provide a new and cheaper commuter route to New York City. The Westchester began at the west end of the New Haven's Harlem River Yard in the Bronx, at Willis Avenue and East 132nd Street and shared tracks with the New Haven for its first 4 miles to West Farms. From there the Westchester's four tracks ran to Mt. Vernon, crossed over the top of the New Haven mainline at Columbus Avenue, and then split, with two tracks going to White Plains and two going to Port Chester. The electrified line had no grade

crossings and 23 elaborate stations, all with high-level platforms. It opened in 1912 to White Plains and New Rochelle. The last 9 miles from New Rochelle to Port Chester, completed in 1929, ran adjacent to the New Haven mainline, accounting for catenary structures that even today span the space of two additional tracks. This railroad never handled sufficient passengers because it was necessary to transfer to the Independent Rapid Transit (IRT) subway line to reach Manhattan destinations. The road ceased operations in 1937 after costing the New Haven at least $50 million, more than a quarter of which would never be accounted for.

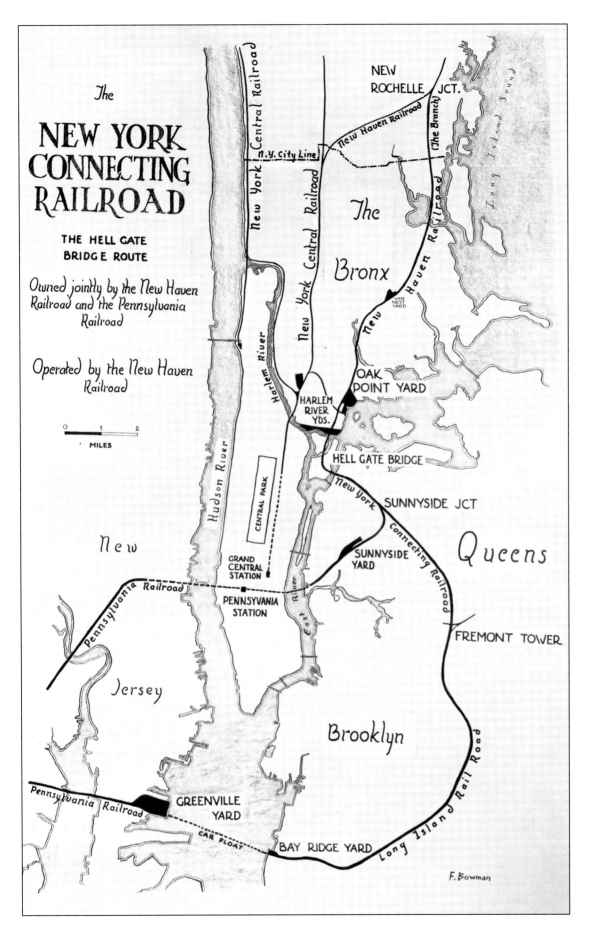

The
NEW YORK CONNECTING RAILROAD

THE HELL GATE BRIDGE ROUTE

Owned jointly by the New Haven Railroad and the Pennsylvania Railroad

Operated by the New Haven Railroad

0   1   2
MILES

NEW ROCHELLE JCT.

New York Central Railroad

N.Y. City Line

New Haven Railroad

(The Branch)

New Haven Railroad

Long Island Sound

The Bronx

New York Central Railroad

VAN NEST YARD

Harlem River

OAK POINT YARD

HARLEM RIVER YDS.

HELL GATE BRIDGE

New York Connecting Railroad

SUNNYSIDE JCT

Central Park

New Jersey

Pennsylvania Railroad

GRAND CENTRAL STATION

Hudson River

East River

PENNSYLVANIA STATION

SUNNYSIDE YARD

Queens

FREMONT TOWER

Brooklyn

Long Island Rail Road

Pennsylvania Railroad

GREENVILLE YARD

CAR FLOAT

BAY RIDGE YARD

F. Bowman

The configuration of New Haven lines and the location of its yards in New York City. A westward New Haven train would head southeast while crossing Hell Gate and then follow an arc of nearly 180 degrees to get into Pennsylvania Station. *Fielding L. Bowman*

29

A 1907 postcard depicts both the new and old bridges across the Connecticut River between Saybrook and Old Lyme. The new double-track bridge was constructed with piers wide enough for two additional tracks.

The elaborate station at Westerly, finished in 1907, served several Rhode Island and Connecticut shore areas such as Watch Hill and Stonington. Numerous Shore Line trains between New York and Boston still stop at Westerly.

N. Y. N. H. & H. Depot, Westerly, R. I.

Providence Union Station, opened in 1899, housed the passenger station, operating headquarters of the Providence Division, and other offices. In the background is the state capitol building.

C 1638.   Union Station, State House and Normal School, Providence, R. I.

Connecting to the mainline at New Rochelle Junction, 16 miles east of Grand Central, was the Harlem River Branch, the New Haven's connection to the west and south. This 11-mile line, which was four-tracked in the 1890s, was expanded from four to six main tracks by 1912. All grade crossings were eliminated, two six-track drawbridges were constructed, and all tracks were electrified. Four new signal towers and 10 elaborate stations for local commuters were constructed. Its two yards in the South Bronx (Oak Point and Harlem River) were enlarged and electrified to allow the transfer of more cars by barge to points around New York City as well as to New Jersey, where connections to railroads operating west and south were made. A large shop for electric locomotives and multiple-unit cars was constructed at Van Nest in the Bronx.

The Harlem River Branch work was done in preparation for the New Haven's last major line construction. The New Haven and the Pennsylvania Railroad formed a joint company, the New York Connecting Railroad, to connect the New Haven with Penn Station, which had opened on 34th Street in Manhattan in 1910. The New York Connecting was a four-track railroad that ascended from the west end of Oak Point Yard in the South Bronx on a viaduct to the Hell Gate Bridge, a huge arch structure that spans the East River between the Bronx and Queens. In 1917, a 5-1/2-mile double-track passenger line was put into service to connect at Harold Tower in Queens to the Pennsylvania's tracks into Penn Station. The New York Connecting, operated and maintained by the New Haven, was electrified. However, New Haven trains to Penn Station had to switch to Pennsy DC locomotives until 1933, when the wire was finally installed from Harold Tower to Penn Station.

In 1894, the year after the Consolidated took over the Shore Line all the way to Boston, there were six through-passenger trains in each direction. Except for the "Five Hour Express," trains normally took six hours to make the journey. In 1894 a portion of the Shore Line east of New Haven was rerouted further inland through the newly constructed East Haven Tunnels, eliminating several road crossings. The same year, the double track on the Shore Line all the way to Boston was completed. Between New Haven and Boston, the railroad was increased to four tracks through Providence—on the 10 miles approaching Boston and in five other locations. In 1913 the New Haven prepared a plan—thwarted by financial problems—to expand to four tracks between Boston and Providence with an electrification system similar to the one west of New Haven. A "Lock and Block" signal system and 58 signal towers were installed on the 157 miles of track between New Haven and Boston. In Connecticut, five new drawbridges were built across the Connecticut, Niantic, Thames, and Mystic Rivers, as well as Shaw's Cove in New London. The town of Westerly, Rhode Island, got a large new station in 1907. Union Station in Providence was completed in 1899, and the huge South Station complex in Boston, completed in 1899, was the terminal for the eastern end of the New Haven's mainline and Old Colony service.

Improving the Infrastructure

To service its growing fleet of steam locomotives, construction of shops at Readville, 9

The East Side Tunnel that took the electrified double-track line from downtown Providence underneath Brown University toward Warren and Bristol just after the wire to Bristol was removed in early 1935. The tracks to the left go east to Boston. The tunnel and the signal tower at Promenade Street, controlling the east end of Providence Station, were completed in 1909. The streamline train is the new *Comet. Bob Liljestrand collection*

miles west of Boston, began in 1901. In 1904, the New Haven opened a major freight classification facility between New York and Boston at Midway, located 5 miles east of New London in Groton, Connecticut. This facility included a large engine house, a hotel for lodging crews between runs, and a facility for icing perishable freight. In anticipation of this yard, a track connection at Groton was constructed north for 6 miles to Allyns Point to connect with the Norwich-Worcester line in 1899, eliminating the need to use the Central Vermont (CV) line on the other side of the Thames. East of Providence, in Pawtucket, Rhode Island, after a battle of several years with that city, the New Haven relocated half a mile of its double-track mainline off of five busy city streets and onto a four-track cut with no road crossings. The New

Haven had threatened to bypass Pawtucket by operating via a newly constructed tunnel to East Providence and the East Junction branch to Attleboro, Massachusetts. The city of Pawtucket finally consented and the new route opened in 1916 with the four new main tracks and a new overhead station known as Pawtucket and Central Falls.

By 1915 the New Haven-Hartford-Springfield line had a new automatic signal system of the semaphore variety, as used on the mainline west of New Haven. This system replaced the antiquated banner or banjo-type signals that had contributed to a disastrous North Haven wreck in 1913 when 21 people were killed. With banner signals, each signal displayed "proceed" or "stop" and had no approach signal. In the 1913 accident, the *Bar Harbor Express* was stopped in a heavy fog

with its last car just beyond a signal when it was struck by the *White Mountain Express*.

As soon as the New Haven assumed control of the Central New England in 1904, it began a massive upgrading project to make the Maybrook line a major east-west freight route. The route, 110 miles to its connection with the mainline at Devon, consisted of parts of five lines: Central New England, New York & New England, the Housatonic mainline, a Housatonic branchline, and the Naugatuck. The bridge across the Hudson River at Poughkeepsie, New York, had already eliminated the need to float freight cars at Fishkill Landing. Large yard and engine house facilities were constructed at Maybrook, and from 1904 to 1906 the New Haven undertook an extensive upgrading and double-tracking project between Maybrook and Danbury. Five

heavy-construction contractors worked simultaneously to expand the right-of-way, strengthen and rebuild bridges, widen cuts, expand fills, improve grades, and eliminate highway crossings. Steep grades and longer mileage had ruled out use of the remote Central New England route east from Poughkeepsie to Hartford, and the NY&NE mainline east of Danbury to Waterbury remained single-track due to its 1.6 percent grades. Instead, the line from Danbury to Derby, the junction with the Naugatuck line, was double-tracked between 1910 and 1913. Even though it was nearly 17 miles longer than the NY&NE, this route used by trains bound for New Haven was also favored for trains going to Waterbury and Hartford because its grades were half those of the NY&NE. On the New Haven, eastward

South Station in Boston soon after it opened in 1899. Steam locomotives waiting to depart were required to stay outside of the train shed. *Bob Liljestrand collection*

33

Above: New Haven President Charles S. Mellen's wife persuaded him to copy the bell tower of Siena, Italy, at the Waterbury, Connecticut, Station. This substantial station also housed the headquarters of the Waterbury Division until they were relocated to Hartford during the depression. *Bob Liljestrand Collection*

Opposite: At West Pawling, New York, a westbound freight headed for Maybrook meets an eastbound destined for Cedar Hill and Boston in 1950. Double-tracking this line before World War I was a great effort considering the fills, cuts, and curves along the line. *Kent Cochrane. Thomas J. McNamara Collection*

grades were of prime importance because eastward trains hauled mostly loaded cars while westward trains handled many empties and needed less power. In addition, automatic signals were installed on the entire Maybrook line, with the final segment completed in 1926.

Along with improvements to its core routes, the New Haven did extensive work on its secondary routes. By World War I, 38 percent of the New Haven's route mileage was double-track, including all but 20 of the 180 miles from Devon, Connecticut, through Waterbury, Hartford, and Willimantic to

Boston. The lines from Providence to Worcester, New Bedford to Framingham, and Boston to Buzzards Bay were also double-tracked, and in 1909 a double-track tunnel was opened in Providence to carry the tracks from downtown Providence, underneath Brown University, to East Providence, Bristol, Rhode Island, and Fall River, Massachusetts.

This line was electrified and operated more than 100 suburban trains per day.

In addition to trackage improvements, in 1909 an elaborate new station in Waterbury—designed to resemble the bell tower in Siena, Italy—was completed. Mellen's wife saw the tower on a trip to Europe and instructed her husband to imitate

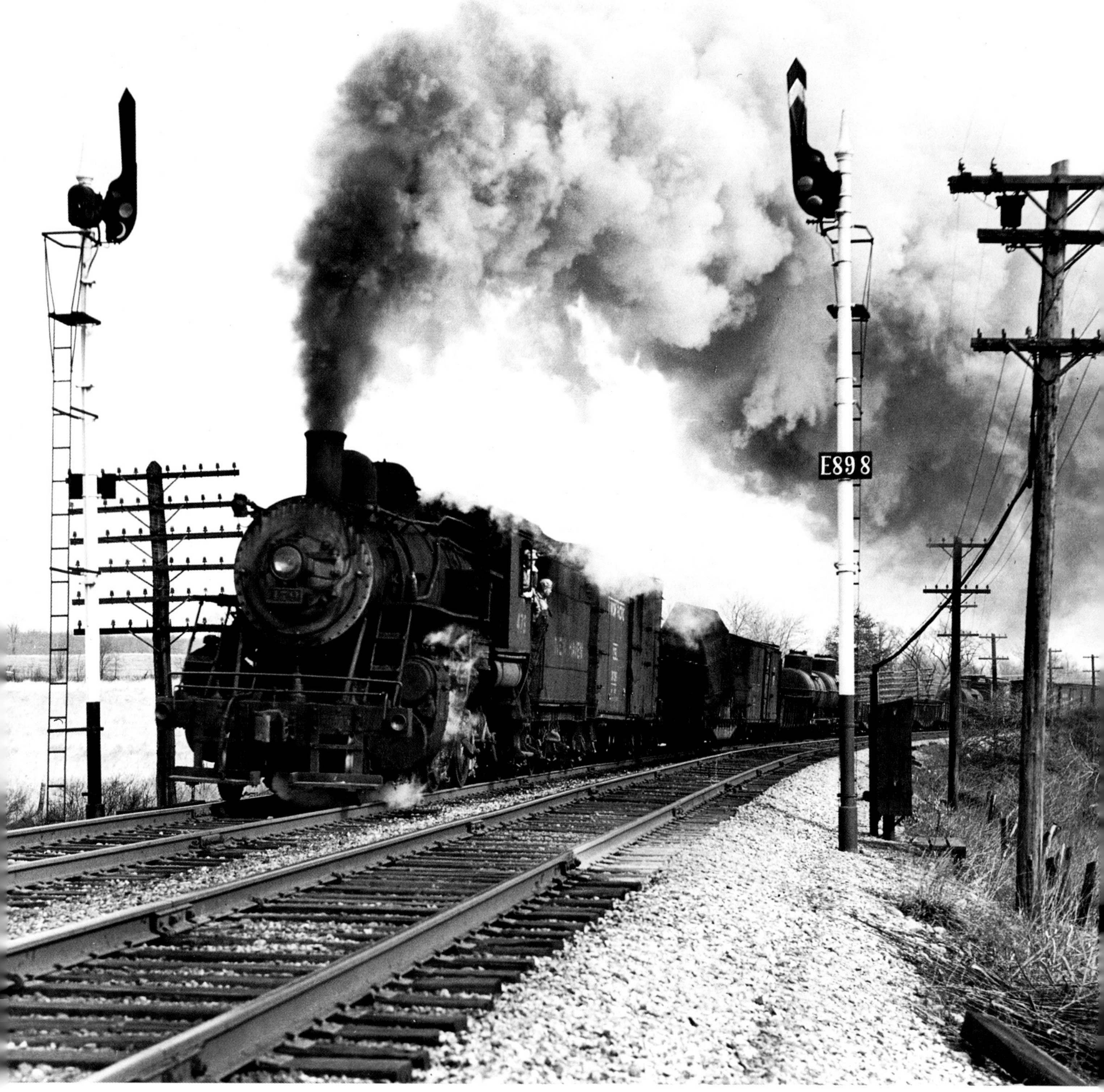
E89 8

it on the railroad. In 1907 the New Haven acquired 41 AC/DC Baldwin-Westinghouse electric passenger locomotives for use between Stamford and Grand Central. New Haven locomotives had to be able to operate both on overhead catenaries and on the New York Central's 600-volt DC third rail between Woodlawn and Grand Central Terminal, making the New Haven's passenger locomotives more complex and expensive. By World War I the New Haven had also purchased 39 electric freight locomotives and 15 electric switchers, also from Baldwin-Westinghouse. Yards and industries along the line were equipped with overhead wires and switched with electric locomotives. To serve the growing residential commuter populations in southwestern Connecticut and Westchester County, New York, the New Haven also acquired 73 electric multiple-unit (MU) cars by 1914. These cars were self-propelled, operated from either end for rapid turnaround, and ran both on overhead AC catenary and DC third rail. The MU cars provided the local service into Manhattan from west of Stamford, stopping at 13 suburban stations in western Fairfield County, Connecticut, and Westchester County, New York.

Increasing Tractive Effort

Between 1895 and World War I, the New Haven acquired more than 800 steam locomotives, many from Rhode Island Locomotive Works in Providence, which in 1902 became part of Alco. The first 229 purchased through 1907 for use on passenger, commuter, and small freight trains consisted of 4-4-2 Atlantics, 4-6-0 Ten-Wheelers, and 4-4-0 Americans. From 1898 to 1910, the New Haven purchased 246 2-6-0 Mogul locomotives for use in through-freight service and sometimes in passenger service. These locomotives, known as K-1s, could haul 25 to 30 cars on most New Haven routes.

Starting in 1907 and ending in 1916, the New Haven acquired 138 4-6-2 Pacifics, which became New Haven's I-1, I-2, I-3, and I-4 classes, relegating the first 229 steam locomotives to branchline, local commuter, and local freight runs. In 1916, the New Haven purchased 33 J-Class 2-8-2 Mikados, which could pull 50 to 60 percent more tonnage than the Moguls and began hauling many of the Maybrook and Shore Line tonnage trains. In 1918, the last year of World War I, 50 Santa Fe 2-10-2 L-1-Class locomotives arrived on the New Haven. Their tractive effort—more than double that of the Mogul—took over the heaviest freight runs, especially on the Maybrook line. Also in this period, the New Haven acquired 142 0-6-0 steam switchers.

Despite all of these infrastructure improvements and locomotive additions, the New Haven was not prepared for World War I and was quickly overwhelmed with congestion. Along with the rest of the nation's railroads, it spent the two years from 1918 to 1920 under federal control of the United States Railroad Administration. The New Haven had three basic problems. First, its freightyards were inadequate, always congested, and unable to classify and forward a sufficient number of cars to keep up with the flow of traffic. Second, the locomotive fleet was unable to haul enough cars to keep the yards fluid. And, third, it turned out that Brandeis had been correct: the railroad was not profitable.

Opposite: After 40 years, 2-6-0 Mogul No. 479 is still on the job in 1947, hauling a local freight from Hartford to New Hartford. It heads west on the Highland and in a few miles at Plainville will go north onto the Canal Line. *Kent Cochrane. Thomas J. McNamara Collection*

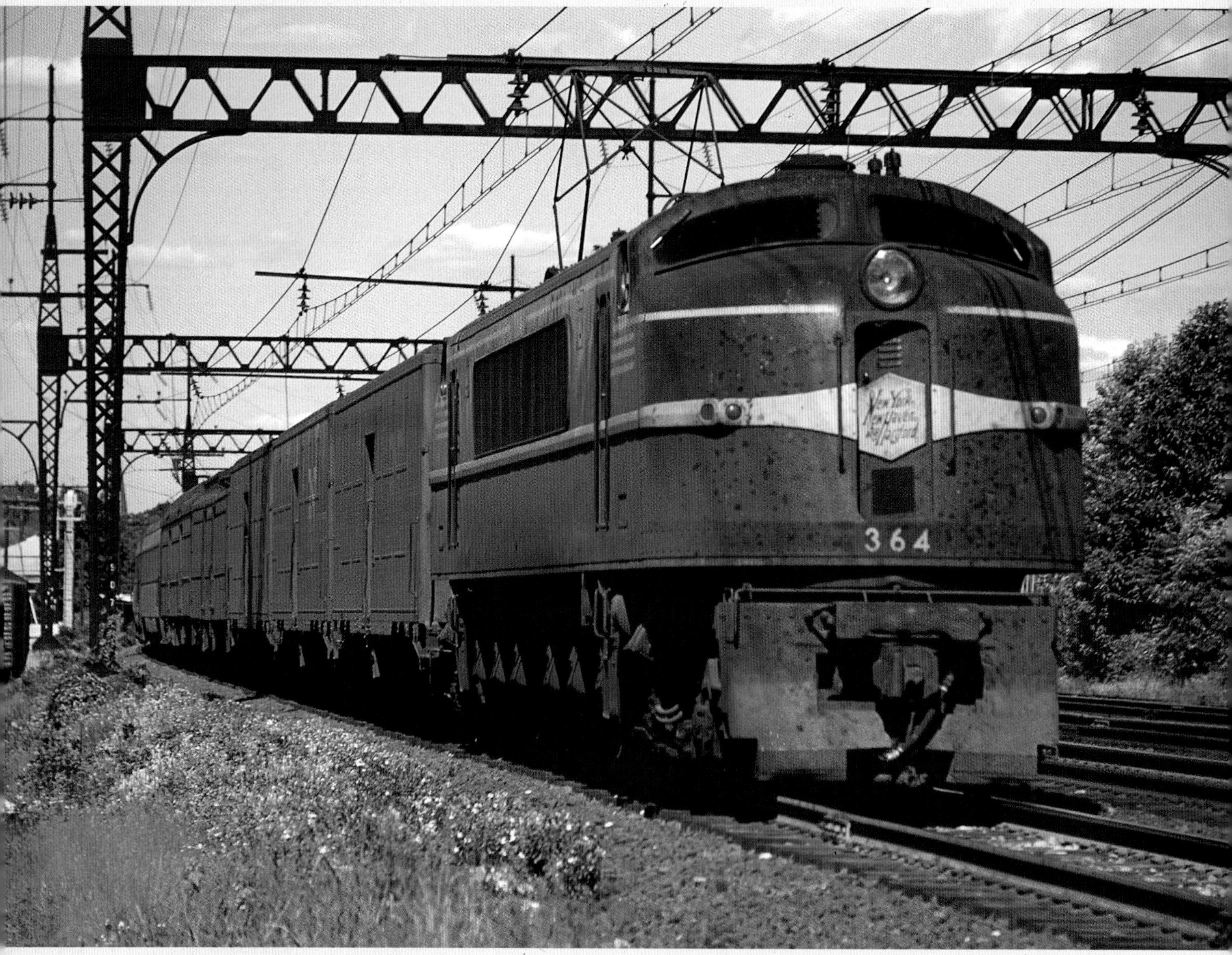
364

CHAPTER THREE

TWO WORLD WARS AND THE DEPRESSION

1918–1945

To address its financial problems and the operating difficulties brought on by World War I, the New Haven made much needed additional infrastructure improvements that, by 1923 would make it profitable.

In 1918 two 8-mile-long freight tracks were completed, connecting to the Long Island Railroad at Fresh Pond Junction in Queens. This permitted New Haven freight trains to continue on an 11-mile Long Island Railroad branch into Brooklyn and Bay Ridge

The streamliners that hauled heavier trains west of New Haven were six GE 3,600-horsepower electrics acquired in 1938. This striking green and gold paint scheme with the script herald would be used subsequently on many road diesels and electrics. In 1957, EP-4 No. 364 heads westward through Milford, Connecticut. *Thomas J. McNamara*

39

Yard, directly across the Hudson River from Greenville Piers, the Pennsylvania Railroad's car-float facility in New Jersey. The float time between Bay Ridge and Greenville was 30 minutes, less than one-third of the time consumed from Oak Point.

In the spring of 1918, however, a huge fire engulfed the New Haven passenger station, which had been built in 1874. An elaborately built four-story brick station opened in 1920. In addition to its large waiting room and concourse, the upper floors had extensive offices to house the New Haven Division operating and engineering staffs. Track capacity at the station was increased from 6 to 10 main tracks, providing 8 platform tracks with 2 freight tracks in the middle. An underground pedestrian tunnel connected the station with the platforms, eliminating the need for passengers to walk across tracks to get on and off the trains.

In the 1920s the New Haven also made significant yard enhancements. Cedar Hill in New Haven was expanded to become the New Haven's major classification facility. It was located east of New Haven Station between the Shore Line and Hartford-Springfield Line. Its eastbound and westbound yards each had three distinct parts for receiving, classification, and departures. Because it was located near the center of the railroad, it could, with one crew, dispatch a train to any significant point on the system. When the expanded yard opened in 1925, it was the largest freightyard east of the Mississippi River, encompassing an area of 1,160 acres. In addition to switching and train make-up tracks, Cedar Hill had a rail-truck

In January 1948, R-2 Mountain 3500, built in 1924, pushes an eastbound Shore Line train through East Haven, Connecticut, to Branford, where it will cut off and return to Cedar Hill. A few months later, pusher service would end with the arrival of more diesels. *Kent Cochrane. Thomas J. McNamara Collection*

transfer station with capacity for 402 cars; two locomotive roundhouses with 72 stalls; a car shop with room for 120 cars; and a tie creosoting plant that annually treated over one million cross ties. Initially, brakemen rode cars over the east and west humps to apply brakes by hand. However, by 1929, pneumatic car retarders were installed on both humps to eliminate this dangerous operation.

Gaining Motive Power

Cedar Hill and expanded yards in Hartford and Providence, also equipped with car retarders in 1929, greatly increased the ability of the New Haven to move much more traffic in an effective manner. With these yards the New Haven could carefully schedule its freight for prompt movement. This discipline provided excellent service and kept the yards

fluid. In the New York area the 1927 extension of the electrification west from Oak Point to Bay Ridge Yard enabled trains from Bay Ridge to be forwarded directly to Cedar Hill without handling at Oak Point. This sped up the service, reduced the use of Midway Yard, and precluded the need to expand Westchester Yard, a holding point 5 miles east of Oak Point for cars that would not fit in Oak Point because of congestion. Also, the 24-mile Danbury branch was electrified in 1925, eliminating the need for Danbury-New York trains to change locomotives at Stamford or South Norwalk.

The acquisition of motive power in the 1920s and 1930s was carefully planned to handle heavy, high-volume passenger and freight trains. From 1919 through 1928 the New Haven purchased 71 Alco 4-8-2

Acquired in 1920, R-1 Mountain 3329 is in Willimantic, Connecticut, during the rough winter of 1947 and 1948. The snow on the engine came from opening up the line from Providence. *Kent Cochrane. Thomas J. McNamara Collection*

The gas-electric self-propelled car replaced steam locomotives on many New Haven branches. In 1948, the 9105 (built in 1926) would make 11 daily roundtrips on the 7.82 miles between North Easton and Canton Junction, where a passenger could catch a Providence local into Boston. *Kent Cochrane. Thomas J. McNamara Collection*

Mountain freight locomotives, primarily for use between Maybrook and Boston. Also purchased were 50 Alco 0-8-0 steam switchers to work the humps and make up trains in large yards like Cedar Hill, Providence, and Hartford. These would be the last steam freight locomotives that the New Haven would acquire. To deal with the rising cost of sharply declining branchline passenger volume, the New Haven purchased 23 rail buses

and gas-electric railcars between 1921 and 1927. These vehicles, with capacities for 34 to 45 passengers on the buses and 65 on the railcars, were used on Central New England lines and Old Colony spur lines that connected to routes from Boston. The gas-electrics could be operated with a smaller crew and quickly headed back for another trip because they did not need to be turned around as did the steam trains.

Between 1919 and 1928 the electric passenger fleet was augmented by the addition of 27 Westinghouse electric locomotives (EP-2 class), which, with twice the horsepower (2,052) of the early units, quickly took over hauling the premium Boston trains and other heavy trains between New York and New Haven. To handle the growing New York City

suburban development, the electric multiple-unit fleet was tripled to more than 200 cars by 1930. The passenger fleet was further enhanced by the 1931 acquisition of 10 General Electric 2,700-horsepower EP-3 units, known as "Flatbottoms," that were assigned to the heaviest trains. Two of these locomotives were borrowed by the Pennsylvania Railroad in the early 1930s and sent to the PRR for testing. The PRR GG-1, with its streamlined carbody, was based on these New Haven units.

In 1929 and 1930 the New Haven added what would become two of its best-known trains. The first was the *Senator*, a midday limited-stop train between Boston and Washington, operated together with the Pennsylvania Railroad. The *Senator*, an

EP-2 Westinghouse passenger electric No. 324 in its original paint scheme hauls a westbound train through Southport, Connecticut, in 1956. *Thomas J. McNamara*

The 10 EP-3 electrics, or "Flatbottoms," that arrived in 1931 became the workhorses that hauled the New Haven's heavy passenger trains. In 1956 the No. 357 heads west through Glenbrook, Connecticut, with a Boston train that will soon stop in Stamford. *Thomas J. McNamara*

extra-fare train with no coaches, left Boston and Washington at 12:30 P.M. with parlor cars, a club car, a dining car, and an observation car. The following year, despite the onset of the Great Depression, the New Haven started the *Yankee Clipper*, leaving Boston and New York at 3:30 P.M., also an extra-fare train without coaches. To trumpet the new trains, the New Haven's March 1930 timetable stated, "Introducing A New Monarch over the Boulevard of Steel…. Throughout this truly de luxe train are provided lavish appointments: specially arranged parlor cars, drawing rooms, and facilities for card playing. Each glistening car will bear some name famous in clipper history." Some of the Pullman cars were christened with heraldic names like *Flying Cloud, Dreadnought, Sovereign of the Seas*, and *Great Republic*. Both the *Senator* and the *Yankee Clipper* would survive the depression, with the *Clipper* in 1933 rescheduled to leave Boston and New York at 1:00 P.M. By 1940 the trains would also have coaches.

The railroad's fixed plant and operation underwent drastic change from 1920 through the early-1930s. Expanded use of the automobile, improvement of highways, and the onset of the depression had a major impact upon New Haven branchline operations. In 1920 the New Haven provided passenger service on all but 71 of its 2,256 route miles. By 1934 passenger service had been dramatically cut from more than 1,000 route miles, including from most branchlines other than those providing Boston or New York commuter service. With this downsizing came a paring of trackage so that by 1938, more than 300 route miles had been abandoned and removed. This was, to a large extent, a correction of earlier overexpansion. The track removals first consisted of more than 180 miles of the Central New England, leaving only the Maybrook-to-Poughkeepsie route and three short segments in Connecticut. The second area of removal involved 80 miles of duplicate, parallel Old Colony routes, the loss of which affected few communities. The third area consisted of small pieces of low-volume branchlines comprising 55 miles of track. In both passenger and freight, the 1930s saw the New Haven concentrate on its core routes. By 1932, the railroad's 10 operating divisions were merged into four: New Haven, Providence, Hartford, and Boston.

These cutbacks, however drastic, were still inadequate to stem the New Haven's financial problems, which increased in the depression years of 1929 through 1933, when revenues dropped 55 percent. The onerous burden of bond interest, principal, and excessive lease payments coming due for the many acquired lines forced the New Haven to declare bankruptcy in 1935 and end the efforts of the Pennsylvania Railroad to take over the New Haven.

The PRR had started acquiring New Haven stock in 1904 and stepped up its acquisition after World War I to try to control service and freight rates in New England in competition with the New York Central's Boston & Albany route. PRR attempts to operate the New Haven, however, were strongly opposed by Massachusetts, Connecticut, and Rhode Island. This opposition combined with the financial complexity of the New Haven's debts and leases and the bankruptcy to thwart the Pennsylvania and render its investment worthless.

Streamlining Operations

Bankruptcy, however, did not deteriorate the operation of the New Haven. In fact, in many areas the railroad began to improve. By 1935 the railroad had eliminated many passenger

The "Aristocrat of Trains" was debuted in this March 18, 1930, timetable. *The Yankee Clipper* was a new all-reserved Pullman parlor car train that ran between Boston and New York.

Starting in 1935, the *Comet*, a three-car streamline train, ran the 44 miles between Providence and Boston in 44 minutes with two stops. It became a victim of its own success when passenger use outgrew the train. In 1948 it was used on Old Colony shuttles such as this one between Braintree and Cohasset, Massachusetts. *Kent Cochrane. Thomas J. McNamara Collection*

trains and abandoned trackage or at least left it dormant. Howard S. Palmer, a New Haven vice president appointed to be one of three trustees as well as president, assembled an innovative group to revitalize the railroad. Relieved through bankruptcy of some debt and lease payments, the new team made a number of important innovations in the late-1930s. The automatic signaling on the Shore Line was completed with the elimination of the Manual Block, or "Lock and Block" signal system and

Above: In 1937 the New Haven acquired its last 10 steam locomotives, Hudson I-5s used to haul heavy passenger trains between New Haven and Boston. In 1948 the *Yankee Clipper* passes Rocky Neck along the Connecticut Shore Line route. *Kent Cochrane. Thomas J. McNamara Collection*

Left: A 1938 Alco "high hood" switcher sits at the end of its career on the scrap line in the Readville Shops in 1958. *Thomas J. McNamara*

In 1938, the New Haven began TOFC (trailer on flatcar) service. In 1956 this electric freight hauls piggybacks west through Green's Farms, Connecticut, on its way to the Harlem River Yard in the South Bronx. *Thomas J. McNamara*

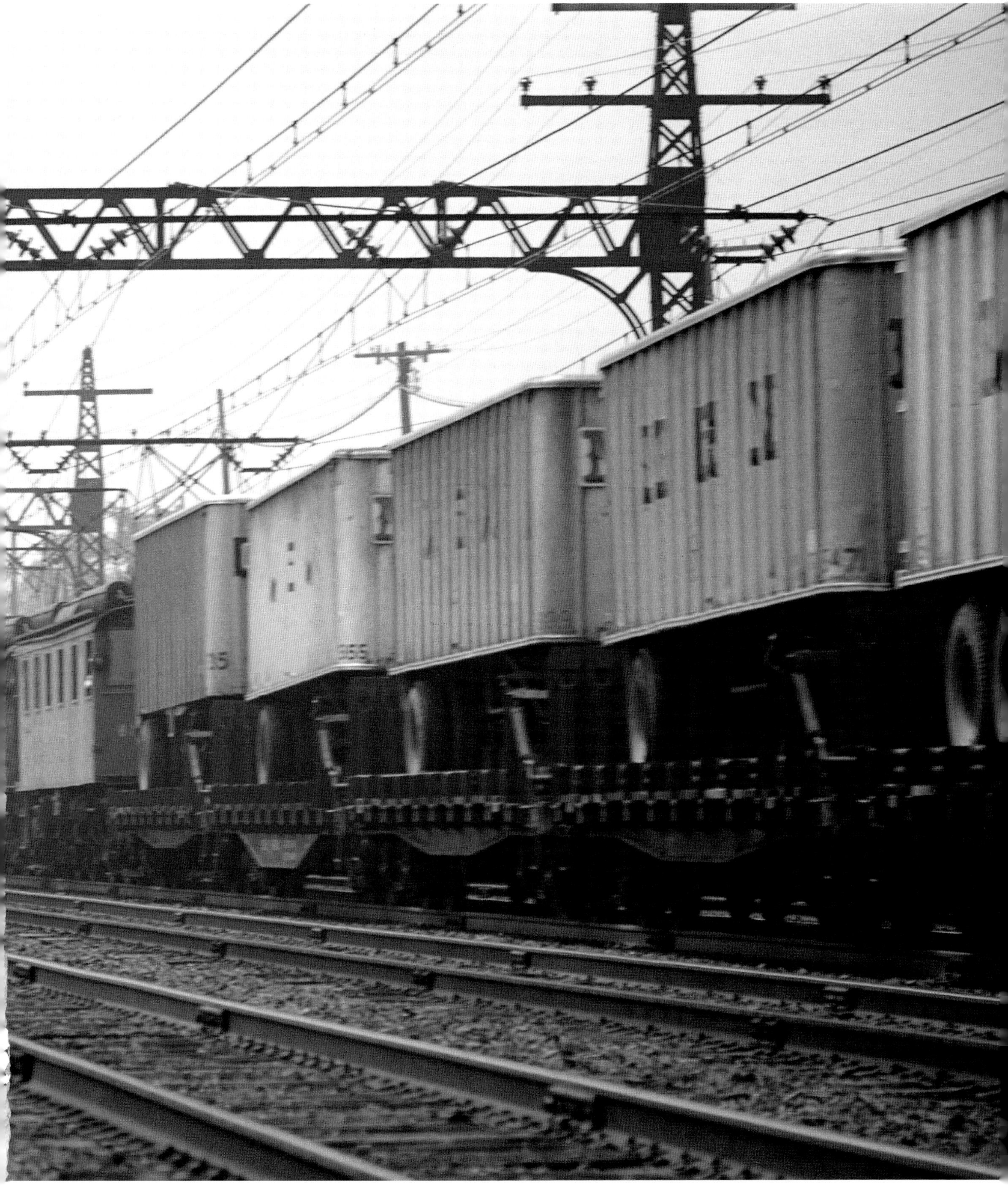

During World War II the New Haven acquired 19 GE 44-ton switchers for its shops and small yards. This one is inside the huge electric locomotive shops at Van Nest in the Bronx in 1954. *Thomas J. McNamara*

the installation of cab signals. This system repeated wayside signal indications on a small panel in the engine cab and was most useful along the Shore Line, especially in the fog.

The New Haven also participated fully in the "streamline" era. In June 1935 the railroad began express service between Boston and Providence with the *Comet*. This three-car, aluminum-sheathed train with 400-horsepower diesel engines at each end was built by Goodyear Zepplin of Akron, Ohio. The cab at each end allowed quick turnaround and the train made five roundtrips, 440 miles total, every day but Sunday. The *Comet* had seats for 160 passengers and made the 44-mile one-way journey in 44 minutes for a fare of 90 cents.

To upgrade the passenger car fleet, the New Haven between 1934 and 1938 purchased 250 American Flyer air-conditioned coaches, built at a Pullman plant on the New Haven in Worcester. To deal with the 12-car limit of an I-4 Pacific on a Shore Line passenger, the railroad acquired 10 streamlined Hudson-class passenger locomotives (I-5 class) from Baldwin in 1937. This power was used on Shore Line trains to meet tight schedules with 16- to 18-car trains, as well as to prevent operation of extra sections. Shortly after their arrival, the Hudsons were handling almost all Shore Line trains between Boston and New Haven, and occasional trains between New Haven and Springfield.

Complementing them was the addition of six General Electric 3,600-horsepower, streamlined, electric passenger locomotives (EP-4s) in 1938 to improve operation between New Haven and New York. With this new equipment and ridership, daily roundtrips between New York and Boston increased from 14 in 1935 to 18 in 1941, providing hourly service between morning and evening with fewer trains at night.

The New Haven was also an early advocate of diesel-powered locomotives. It purchased an Alco test switcher in 1931 and by 1940 had purchased a total of 30: 10 from GE and 20 from Alco. Another innovation of the late 1930s was piggyback service. While this did not begin to develop on most railroads until the 1950s, the New Haven in 1938 began hauling trailers on flatcars between Boston, Providence, and its Harlem River terminal in the Bronx. To enhance its passenger business, the New Haven also established its "rail-auto" plan, which allowed travelers to rent cars at the major stations. This service was available at 13 locations: six key points along the Shore Line, plus Hartford, Springfield, Pittsfield, Worcester, and three stations on the Old Colony.

The approach of World War II found the New Haven system much better prepared for vast traffic increases (total revenue in 1943 was three times that of 1933) due to the expe-

At Readville, several idle locomotives wait either for the war or the torch in this stark 1932 photo. Some would be cut up, while others, such as T-Class switcher 2393, would be reactivated between 1939 and 1942. *Charles A. Brown. J. W. Swanberg Collection*

Between 1941 and 1945 the New Haven acquired 60 of these 2,000-horsepower Alco DL-109 road diesels to haul Shore Line and Springfield passenger trains by day and freight trains at night. These units ended their days on commuter runs like this 1958 Boston–Providence local heading west through Sharon, Massachusetts. *Thomas J. McNamara*

rience acquired by its employees, the upgrades made to the major routes and yards, and the availability of motive power. The severe declines in traffic during the depression had led the railroad to store many of its steam locomotives at the Readville Shops. As traffic significantly increased in 1939 and 1940, locomotives that had been dead for years were drawn back into service to move additional

Right: To expedite wartime tonnage in 1942 and 1943, the New Haven acquired 10 of these 4,860-horsepower EF-3 locomotives, half from GE and half from Baldwin. In 1949 one of the EF-3s hauls a westbound freight headed for Bay Ridge through Green's Farms, Connecticut. *Kent Cochrane. Thomas J. McNamara Collection*

Below: Starting in 1947 these bright orange RS-2 and 3 road switchers replaced steam on the Berkshire Line, where this passenger train heads north from Danbury to Pittsfield in 1955 at Cornwall Bridge, Connecticut. *Thomas J. McNamara*

In 1948 and 1949, 27 new 2,000-horsepower Alco PAs began displacing the New Haven's Hudson steam locomotives and DL-109s from Shore Line trains. This train with white flags was an advance section running westbound at Pine Orchard on Washington's Birthday in 1956. *Thomas J. McNamara*

freight and passenger traffic. To deal with war traffic, the New Haven used its existing steam fleet but after acquiring the 10 Hudson passenger locomotives in 1937, never purchased another steam locomotive. Instead, during the 1940s, the New Haven acquired 87 Alco switchers and 60 DL-109s, 2,000-horsepower Alco road diesels. The DL-109s were used on many Shore Line trains and saw maximum utilization—a pair might make a roundtrip on the Shore Line between Boston and New Haven during the daytime and then haul freight at night. Ten new 4,860-horsepower electric-freight locomotives were also purchased—five from Baldwin-Westinghouse in 1942 and five from GE in 1943. A single unit could haul any freight train between Cedar

Hill Yard in New Haven and Oak Point or Bay Ridge, often making several trips per day. The five Baldwins were soon equipped with steam boilers and also hauled passenger trains into Penn Station, but because they were not DC-equipped, they could not enter Grand Central. These additional locomotives helped the New Haven move freight, regular passenger trains, and extensive troop trains over its system during the war.

The End of Steam

In the postwar years the New Haven pushed rapidly to complete the shift to diesel operation and by 1951 the road had acquired 27 Alco PAs (2,000-horsepower); 50 Alco FA freight diesels, including 20 "B" units; and

84 diesel road switchers (74 Alco RS-1/RS-2/RS-3s and 10 Fairbanks-Morse units). Within a few weeks of the 1947 arrival of the first road switchers and FA units, the Maybrook, Waterbury, and Berkshire lines became almost entirely diesel-operated, allowing the railroad to shut down extensive maintenance, coal, and watering facilities. Once the PA locomotives arrived in 1948 and 1949, steam disappeared entirely from regular Shore Line service. Some comparative statistics best illustrate this rapid shift to diesel power. In 1941, for example, the New Haven had 521 active steam locomotives. By the fall of 1949, there were just 171 steamers on the roster. Of those 171, only 45 were actually in service, with the rest in shop status or stored dead to save fuel. By 1949 the only place New Haven steam was found was east of Providence, primarily on the Old Colony trains. By early 1952, a time when most American roads were just beginning to replace steam with diesel power, the New Haven was finished with steam except for an occasional excursion.

While the RS-3s were taking over branchline passenger trains and local freights, 50 Alco FA diesels (30 A and 20 B Units) displaced steam from Maybrook and Shore Line freights. In 1950 a train heads west to Maybrook through Green Haven, New York, with its original orange paint scheme. *Thomas J. McNamara*

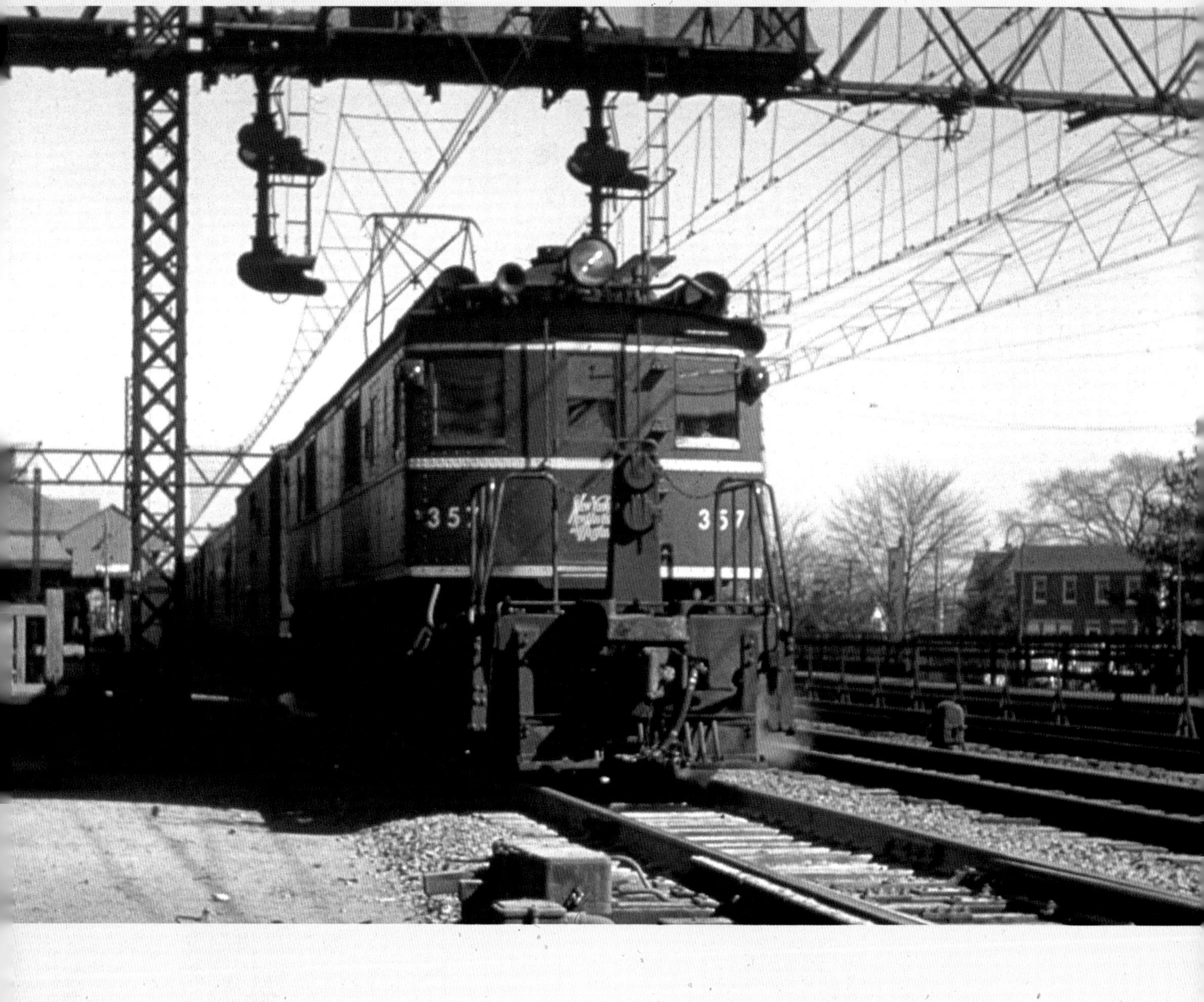
357

CHAPTER FOUR

NEW HAVEN DIVISION

Part I

The West End

The New Haven Division was known as the "West End" of the New Haven Railroad, the mainline from New Haven to its connection with the New York Central Railroad at Woodlawn in the Bronx. This section of the railroad was a four-track, 70-mile-per-hour mainline except for the 1-mile approach to the New York Central between South Mount Vernon and Woodlawn, where it narrowed to three tracks. On the 12 miles from Woodlawn to Grand Central Terminal in Manhattan, New Haven trains operated

A westbound train leaving Stamford in the mid-1950s hauled by EP-3 No. 357. At the opposite end of Stamford Station on the north side was the west end of the New Canaan Branch, and on the south side was the yard and shop facility. *Charles W. Schrade. J. W. Swanberg Collection*

on the four-track New York Central mainline under an 1848 trackage agreement which allowed the New Haven to use half of the terminal. Costs, both of construction and operation, were to be shared based upon the number of cars each road brought into Grand Central Terminal.

Between 1895 and 1907 a British-style signal system, known on the New Haven as "Controlled Manual Block" or "Lock and Block," was installed on the four-track mainline, along with 33 signal towers spaced 2 to 4 miles apart. The tower operators controlling the railroad had to obtain a mechanical unlock from the next tower ahead in order to display a proceed signal. By World War I the Lock and Block system was eliminated along with 13 signal towers and replaced with color-light automatic semaphore signals. The signals were unique to the New Haven because they were left-handed, designed to operate clear of the catenary wires. This signal system,

with the interlockings controlled by the remaining signal towers, provided the New Haven with the ability to move a high volume of passenger and freight traffic over the route. The two outside local tracks were used by passenger trains making local stops and local freight trains serving industries along the line. The two inside express tracks were used by passenger trains making limited stops as well as by through-freight trains. Non-stop passenger trains would sometimes be routed to an outside track to pass slower freight trains.

Sixteen miles east of Grand Central was New Rochelle Junction. At the "Junction," as it was commonly known on the New Haven, the Harlem River Branch diverged to the southwest. The "Branch" was a four-track (six tracks from New Rochelle to Oak Point until the mid 1930s), electrified 70-mile-per-hour line to the South Bronx, Penn Station, and Bay Ridge. At this point the "Penn" jobs—trains to and from the Pennsylvania

Railroad—left or entered the mainline. All freight trains used the Harlem River Branch; some originated or terminated at the two freightyards in the South Bronx, Harlem River, or Oak Point yards, and others went via the Hell Gate Bridge to Bay Ridge.

The busiest section on the New Haven mainline was the 33 miles from Grand Central to Stamford, Connecticut. This stretch had nearly every type of railroading. There were hourly through-trains to Boston

Train No. 177, the *Senator*, crosses the mainline and heads west to Penn Station, hauled by one of the wartime freight-electrics equipped for AC passenger operation. The New Haven was precise in its operations. In 1953, No. 177 was due by New Rochelle Junction at 2:53 P.M.—the time shown by the clock on the sign in the background. *Fielding L. Bowman*

A westbound train heads through Greenwich, Connecticut, toward New York in 1957. The triangular catenary on this section between Stamford and Woodlawn, New York, was the earliest type installed from 1905 to 1907.
Thomas J. McNamara

and Springfield in each direction all day long, and sleeper trains to Washington, Philadelphia, Pittsburgh, Montreal, and northern New England at night. Mail and express trains dropped off or picked up cars. Many through-freight trains traveled through Stamford, where some dropped off or picked up cars. Stamford Yard, with a limited-capacity shop and locomotive facility, was the primary origin point for the New Haven's multiple-unit commuter service. Stamford had a small freightyard with some industry and originated a local freight train to serve nearby industries along the mainline and New Canaan Branch. The New Canaan

Branch was a single-track, Manual Block line extending 8 miles through Springdale to New Canaan. In the morning, the New Canaan branchline had two through-trains to New York that returned in the evening. All day long this line had hourly shuttle trains, provided by one or two electric multiple-unit cars that connected with New York trains in Stamford.

Eight miles east of Stamford is South Norwalk, the junction for the Danbury Branch north to Danbury and the Berkshires. South Norwalk also had a small freightyard, located on the Danbury Branch, known as the Dock Yard. A switching crew worked

Stainless steel multiple-unit cars acquired in 1954 were known as the new "Mutts." In 1957 a westbound local is about to be met by an eastbound train headed for New Haven near Greenwich. *Thomas J. McNamara*

61

Above: In 1954 an electric switcher awaits its next work in Stamford Yard. These locomotives performed most of the yard and local freight switching west of New Haven. *Arthur E. Mitchell*

Left: By 1914 the New Haven completed the installation of catenary wire east of Stamford. For a short section through Glenbrook, 14 of these arch structures were used. In 1956 rectifier-electric No. 377 hauls a New Haven–New York local. *Thomas J. McNamara*

there and also served industries on the Wilson Point Branch, a spur that at one time connected Danbury and Norwalk to waterfront piers on Long Island Sound. The single-track Danbury Branch, extending 24 miles north from South Norwalk and electrified until 1961, was part of the New York City commuter network. Danbury had three pairs of commuter trains, south trains in the morning that returned north in the evening: two to New York City ran through to Grand Central and one to South Norwalk, providing a New York connection. This commuter service was supplemented by two daily roundtrips to Pittsfield, Massachusetts, on the Berkshire Line. This line had some local industry and, until the mid-1950s, an electric locomotive-

hauled freight train between Oak Point Yard in the Bronx and Danbury.

Fourteen miles east of South Norwalk lays the city of Bridgeport, an important passenger stop, as well as a connecting point for Waterbury Branch trains. Just west of Bridgeport Station was the "Lower Yard," formerly the starting point for the Housatonic Railroad. The Lower Yard handled local industry, and for a time received unit coal trains for the United Illuminating Company powerplant. At the western end of the passenger station a spur track headed north to serve some of North Bridgeport's local freight customers. Track beyond that town was removed in 1938 with the abandonment of the southern end of the old

Two FL-9 diesels haul a westbound train through Green's Farms, Connecticut, in 1958. The massive catenary structure next to the signal tower was known as an "anchor bridge." All of the apparatus on top allows the power to be turned off on various sections of track to accommodate repair work. *Thomas J. McNamara*

63

The westbound *Senator* from Boston to Washington heads through Southport, Connecticut, in September 1957. Built in 1931, the EP-3 electric locomotive has been freshly painted in the "McGinnis" scheme. *Thomas J. McNamara*

Housatonic Railroad. At East Bridgeport, electrified freightyards on both sides of the mainline served the considerable heavy industry that once dominated the city. Six miles east of Bridgeport at Devon, formerly Naugatuck Junction, the Waterbury and Maybrook trains left the mainline and headed north.

The terminus of the West End was New Haven, the center and headquarters of New Haven Railroad operations. The station at New Haven, with eight platforms and two through-freight tracks, was always busy. The trains operating east of New Haven changed locomotives at the station, switching between electric and steam or diesel power. These trains also added or dropped passenger, mail, and express cars. Adjacent to the station tracks were storage tracks for passenger trains, electric locomotive facilities, shop facilities, post office tracks, and numerous freight customers

served from Water Street Yard. Two miles east of New Haven Station at Mill River Junction, the Hartford–Springfield line and the Shore Line to Providence and Boston split. Between those two lines, Cedar Hill Yard extended almost five miles north.

The West End served numerous purposes. It was New England's link to New York City. The intercity route between New York, Providence, and Boston was one of the busiest in America. At one time the New Haven, together with the Boston & Maine, operated trains between New York and every significant point in northern New England. It also had heavy through-freight traffic and considerable local industry. The traffic pattern on the West End was varied and dense. Most New York–Boston trains operated in and out of Grand Central. Those en route to Washington, D.C., operated to and from

A pair of ex-Virginian electrics haul a freight train for Cedar Hill, while a westbound passenger train stops at Bridgeport in 1965. *Peter McLachlan*

Penn Station via the Branch. The hourly Boston trains made stops at Stamford and Bridgeport and some made no stops between New Haven and New York City. Hartford–Springfield line trains—also hourly all day long—generally made some of the major stops east of Stamford, such as Darien, South Norwalk, Westport, Fairfield, Bridgeport, and Milford. Also out of New Haven were many locomotive-hauled trains that moved commuters from points between New Haven and Stamford to Grand Central. Many of these trains had 12 to 16 cars, including a bar car, which served a large number of passengers en route home and thus created a challenge for many conductors seeing that passengers disembarked at the correct stations. The New Haven mainline was a very high-density commuter line. For example, for years Number 367 from New Haven to New York City with 16 cars would pick up 700 commuters at just one stop, Westport, Connecticut, every morning.

Commuter Growth

West of Stamford, the traffic density was much greater because of the multiple-unit commuter service. All day long there was half-hourly service between New York and the local stations. During the morning and evening rush hours, each station had service every 15 to 20 minutes with the volume of traffic so great that most of the rush-hour trains would make only three or four of the 13 stops west of Stamford, requiring the operation of many trains. Throughout the twentieth century, commuter service along the New Haven grew considerably. The Westchester County suburbs in New York had a tremendous boom in large, upscale houses in the years before and after World War I. In the 1920s this growth extended into the Connecticut coastal suburbs, known locally as the "Gold Coast." Not only did the commuter trains have bar cars, several had private club cars. These "members only" cars required an additional monthly fee and were staffed with attendants

The expansive track
layout forms the
eastern end of New
Haven. The station is
the brick structure in
the background. The
short "relay" tracks
were used to change
from electric to
diesel power. This
DL-109-hauled train
is about ready to
leave for Boston in
1949. *Kent
Cochrane. Thomas J.
McNamara Collection*

who served drinks. For many years some of
the rush-hour trains originated and terminated in small yards in East Port Chester and
New Rochelle, New York, but in 1958 and
1959 all of the trains were extended to start
and stop in Stamford.

The New Haven's commuter service on
the West End was unique in many ways. All
of its business was concentrated on one route
with two feeder lines to New Canaan and
Danbury. Its travel into and out of New York
City, although concentrated in the morning
and evening rush hours, was substantial in
both directions from 6 A.M. until midnight.
The New Haven always had substantial
reverse commuting—that is, many people
who lived in New York City commuted to
work in Westchester County or Connecticut

destinations. In the later years, a number of
large corporations moved their headquarters
to the Stamford area, creating another commuter destination. This line also had very
heavy ridership between local stations, such as
students going to school and commuters
going to work a few towns away. The New
Haven was also heavily used on weekends and
weekday evenings for leisure travel to New
York City.

In addition to its numerous passenger
trains, the West End handled 20 to 25 electri-
cally hauled freight trains a day. Some
through-freight trains were scattered throughout the daytime, but many more ran at night
along with the sleeper and mail trains. East of
Devon the New Haven operated another 15 to
20 freight trains, the steam- or diesel-hauled

A northbound
Berkshire train
approaches Wilton
Station on the
Danbury Branch in
1954. *Thomas J.
McNamara*

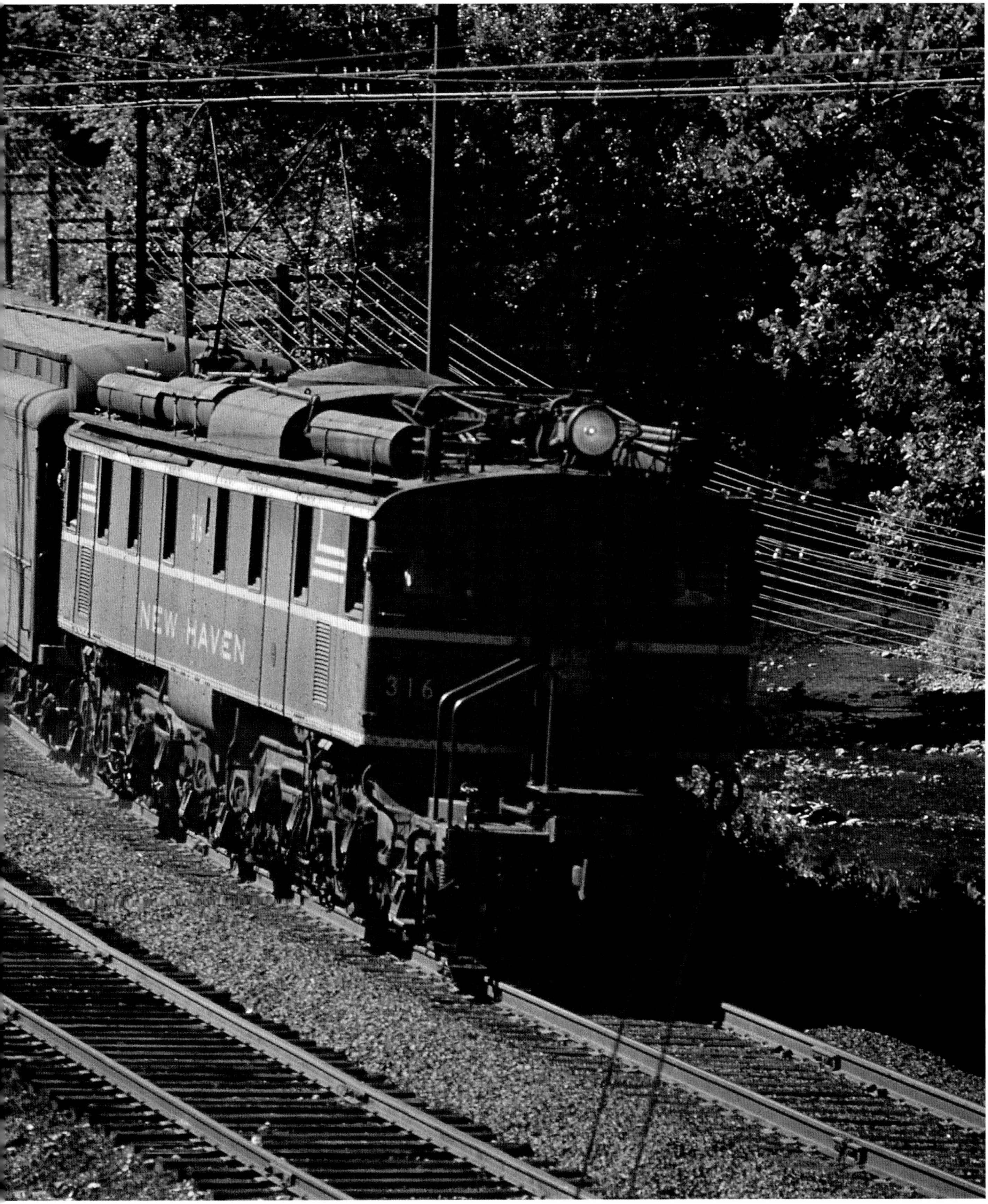
NEW HAVEN
316

Above: The "Dink," a one- or two-car shuttle that ran back and forth every hour to Stamford, awaits its next departure from New Canaan, Connecticut, in 1947. Liquor and Broadway show advertisements at every station provided extra revenue. *Kent Cochrane. Thomas J. McNamara Collection*

Right: The "Jitney" shuttled employees back and forth between Cedar Hill Yard and New Haven Station several times a day. The three cars were previously open-platform MU trailer cars. This train, stopped at Mill River Junction where the Shore Line and Hartford Lines split, was discharging employees on their way home. This I-2 Pacific was 30 years old and in its last months of service in late 1947. *Kent Cochrane. Thomas J. McNamara Collection*

Headed up the rural Danbury branch in Georgetown is train No. 140, bound for Pittsfield at the end of the Berkshire Line in 1949. The Westinghouse electric is in its original 1927 paint scheme. *Kent Cochrane. Thomas J. McNamara Collection*

Waterbury or Maybrook trains. The New Haven also used electric freight-switching locomotives. The yards along the West End were all equipped with overhead catenary to power the locomotives. Likewise, local industries were also switched with electric locomotives since industrial spurs also had overhead catenary wire. The fireman operated a switch to turn the power on when entering an industry's track and shut it off when finished. From the late-1920s until the mid-1950s it was unusual to see a non-electric train in these capacities except for the "Wire Train," which performed catenary maintenance and needed the power shut off in order to work.

The West End was a substantially built line that remained almost unchanged for half of a century from World War I until the end of the New Haven. Other than color light signals replacing semaphores west of Stamford in 1947 and the construction of Interstate 95 alongside of it for miles, the railroad looked about the same in 1968 as it did in 1918.

The "Wire Train" and its personnel performed maintenance and inspections on the catenary system. The tower car that could be raised and lowered provided a platform for power department workers to make adjustments and repairs. The pantograph on the boxcar behind the engine grounded the dead wire, requiring a steam or diesel locomotive to move the train. This train is working in front of Danbury Station in 1947. *Kent Cochrane. Thomas J. McNamara Collection*

71

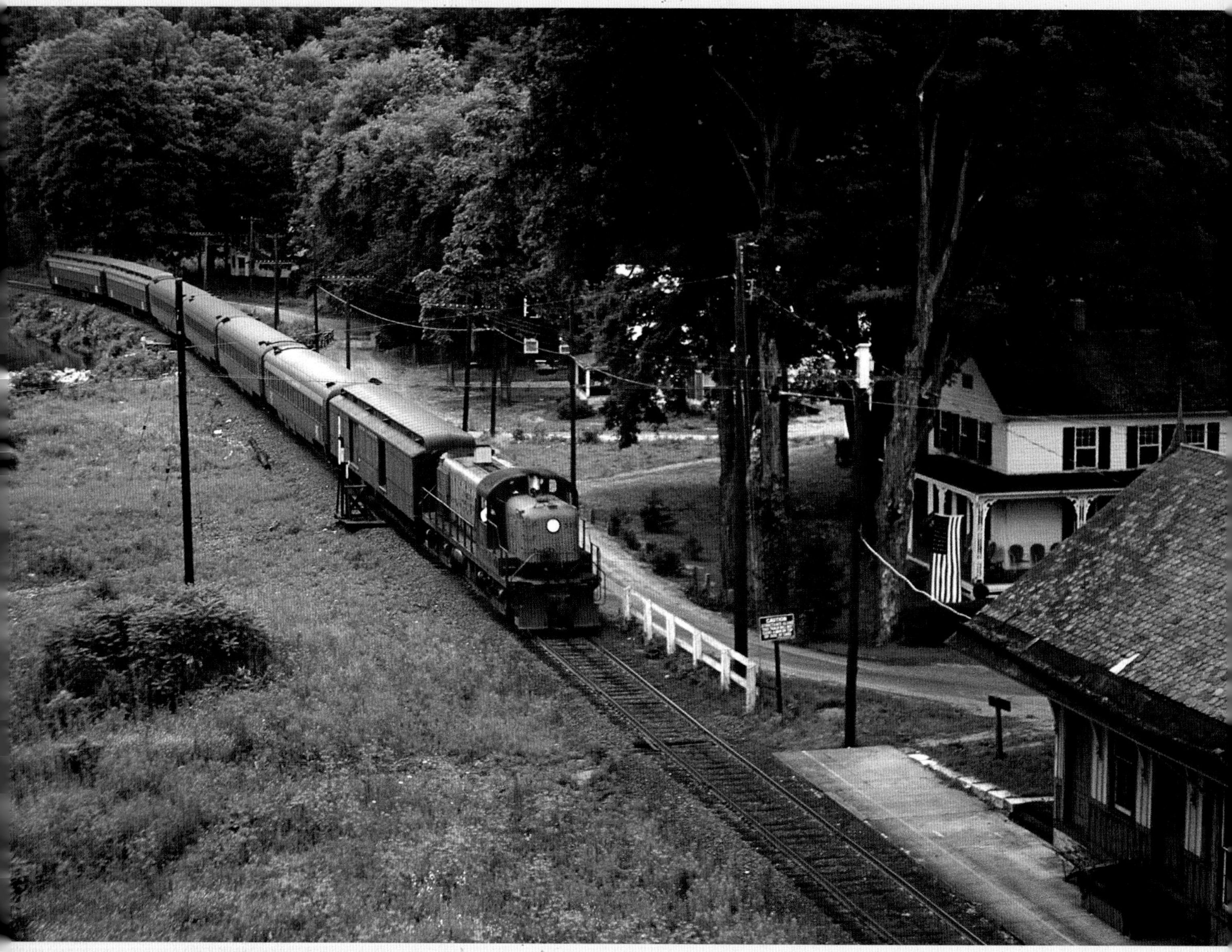

CHAPTER FIVE

NEW HAVEN DIVISION

Part II

Where the Milk Trains Ran

In early 1932 the New Haven Division absorbed the Danbury Division, which until 1927 had been the Danbury Division and Central New England Railway. This territory consisted of just over 430 miles of former Housatonic and the Central New England lines. With the CNE, the New Haven was saddled with a large network of light-density lines in western Connecticut and eastern New York. In 1920 the Danbury Division operated more than 50 weekday passenger trains, with one or two roundtrips on every line.

On a Sunday afternoon in 1956, train No. 145 arrives at Cornwall Bridge Station to pick up passengers bound for New York City. *Thomas J. McNamara*

There were commuter trains between Danbury and Litchfield, Waterbury and Bridgeport; two daily trains in each direction between Poughkeepsie and Hartford, with one continuing through to Boston; and local service from Millerton, New York, to Hartford, plus Rhinecliff and Beacon in New York. The 1920s and the depression were extremely hard on this service. Steam-hauled trains were first replaced by gas-electric rail-cars and then discontinued so that by 1933 the only passenger service that remained in this territory was that between Pittsfield, Danbury, and New York City.

Until 1925 this rural territory had a regular milk run. In 1920, train No. 573 began the six-hour daily run (just over two hours for a passenger train) south on the Berkshire Line from Pittsfield, Massachusetts, toward Danbury. At all the stations along the way it picked up loaded cans of milk. At Canaan, where the CNE crossed the Berkshire, train No. 573 spent more than an hour picking up milk cars from CNE trains that arrived from Hartford and Poughkeepsie, New York, which had gathered milk from points in Connecticut and New York. From Danbury, No. 573 became freight-run QH-1 and operated to Harlem River Yard in the Bronx, providing morning delivery in New York City. Cars with empty milk cans returned north in regular freight service. The milk run lasted until 1925; milk was handled by local freight service for a few more years until trucks took it over.

Eastbound freight on the east approach of the Poughkeepsie Bridge in 1954. The train is hauled by two FA units with a B Unit in the middle. *Thomas J. McNamara*

The Maybrook and the Berkshire Lines

Of the Danbury Division's 430 route miles, fewer than 200 were useful to the New Haven. The Maybrook Line was a heavy-tonnage freight route and, until the very end of the New Haven in late 1969, had six through-trains in each direction every day. The double-track Maybrook Line extended just over 100 miles from Berea, the east end of Maybrook Yard, through Danbury to Derby Junction, where it joined the Naugatuck Line from Waterbury to Devon. From Derby Junction a freight train could either head north to Waterbury and Hartford, or south to Devon to enter the mainline to go to Cedar Hill Yard in New Haven, and then on to Providence and Boston.

A line from New York City via South Norwalk joined the Maybrook Line at Danbury Station. For three miles the Berkshire and Maybrook Lines shared the double track to Berkshire Junction, where the 86-mile Berkshire Line branched off to the north and Pittsfield, Massachusetts. The Berkshire Line,

Above: L-1 Santa Fe type (2-10-2) No. 3223 nears the end of its career in helper service at Hopewell Junction, New York, in 1947. Within a year, FAs would replace steam and eliminate the need to push eastbound trains over the summit at Reynolds. These L-1s arrived on the New Haven at the end of World War I and ran mostly on the Maybrook Line, being considered too slow for Shore Line service. *Kent Cochrane. Thomas J. McNamara Collection*

Below: At Satan's Kingdom, this local freight is near the end of a Canal Line branch and will soon enter CNE territory. The train has just switched the hatchet and axe factory in Collinsville and will now work in Pine Meadow and New Hartford, Connecticut, on the old CNE. *Thomas J. McNamara*

At Berkshire Junction signal station 199 on a Saturday afternoon in 1947, an I-2 Pacific hauls train No. 142 over the switches splitting the double-track Maybrook Line and the single-track Berkshire. This train, with a Pullman parlor car and a diner behind the baggage car, left New York just after 1 P.M., convenient for office personnel in a time when most still worked until noon on Saturday. *Kent Cochrane. Thomas J. McNamara Collection*

which had enough freight industry for three local freight crews, served a number of purposes. It was an important freight route because of its interchange with the Boston & Albany Division (B&A) of the New York Central Railroad. This interchange, located on the New York-Massachusetts border at the end of the 10-mile State Line Branch from Pittsfield, joined the Berkshire at Rising, just north of Great Barrington. Until 1959, State Line was the largest interchange between the New Haven and the New York Central. A daily freight between Danbury and State Line moved traffic that was distributed on various trains from Danbury. After several derailments along this branch, however, the interchange was relocated to Pittsfield in 1959. This arrangement lasted until late 1960 when, in a move that foreshadowed the Penn Central takeover of the New Haven, cars were rerouted to the Oak Point, Springfield, Worcester, or Framingham interchange, depending upon the car's destination.

On Sunday morning two I-2s await the arrival of train No. 138 from New York. Here at Danbury in 1947 these two Pacifics will take over after the electric cuts off. The two engines will be split in Pittsfield for two evening trains to bring weekenders back to New York. *Kent Cochrane. Thomas J. McNamara Collection*

The Berkshire also moved a number of large transformers manufactured at the General Electric plant in Pittsfield. Although this plant was located on the B&A, many transformers, because of their size, were moved on the New Haven to Danbury and then on to Maybrook, where they were routed westward on the Erie Railroad because of the route's greater clearance capacity.

Morgan and Mellen also had plans for the Berkshire as a route to Montreal via

In 1956, IR-1 hauls tonnage from the B&A at State Line, Massachusetts. This train, running along the east bank of the scenic Housatonic River, will arrive in Danbury in about an hour. There, its cars will be forwarded east or west on Maybrook Line trains. *Thomas J. McNamara*

A southbound freight from State Line passes the 1872 depot in Canaan, Connecticut, in 1947. R-1a 3323 has just crossed the diamond of the CNE west to Lakeville and east to some local industries in Canaan. In a few months RS3s will replace steam on this line. *Kent Cochrane. Thomas J. McNamara Collection*

connection to the B&A's Pittsfield-North Adams branch, the B&M and the Rutland. In 1911 the New Haven acquired a large portion of Rutland stock. Because this idea occurred as financial and political woes were mounting, and as B&M control was slipping away, the endeavor did not succeed. However, the Berkshire right-of-way did receive a number of improvements in anticipation of much more traffic. In 1913 the first 11 miles from Berkshire Junction to New Milford were double-tracked and some line relocations made to straighten the track and eliminate highway crossings. New bridges of substantial stone construction indicated a line of some importance.

The Berkshire was also an important passenger route for the New Haven. The Berkshire Mountains of western Connecticut and especially Berkshire County in Massachusetts was a resort and weekend area heavily patronized by New Yorkers. In the 1890s, many influential New York businesspeople had 40- to 50-room "cottages" built in the Berkshires as summer and weekend retreats. Great Barrington, Stockbridge, and Lenox, Massachusetts, each had an elaborate stone station with a *porte cochere* to protect important passengers moving between their carriages and Pullman or private railcars. New Haven President Charles Mellen had an elaborate estate in Stockbridge.

The service pattern on the Berkshire Line remained the same for decades, with two daily roundtrips between Pittsfield and New York City, and additional weekend trains. The morning southbound and the evening northbound trains were known as the *Berkshire*. These trains had a dining car, and on Fridays the northbound *Berkshire* had a reserved-seat parlor car that returned on Sunday evening.

An important financial addition to this service was a Railway Post Office (RPO) car on all four trains except on Sundays. RPOs brought all mail in and out of the region for years until January 1960, when the U.S. Postal Service terminated the New Haven's contract. Soon after, a single Budd rail diesel car (RDC) between Danbury and Pittsfield replaced all but two of the weekend roundtrips.

Stockbridge, Massachusetts, was the country home of New Haven President Charles S. Mellen; the city's elaborate 1905 station was designed by the firm of noted architect Sanford White. Sunday train No. 138 comes to a stop there in 1965. *George E. Ford*

The Berkshire was one of the most scenic lines in New England. Starting in the 1930s the New Haven began to promote excursion travel on the line, and in 1935 began running Sunday ski trains to Norfolk, Connecticut, located east of Canaan, on a short remnant of the Central New England. Soon, more trains to Pittsfield brought skiers to the Berkshires and were credited for making skiing much more popular and available to New Yorkers. The New Haven even produced a film, *Snow Trains of 1936: A Drama of Sports and Transportation*, to advertise its service, which not only provided transportation but a place to eat, drink, and get warm between ski runs. According to *Along the Line*, the New Haven's employee newspaper, the railroad carried 4,000 skiers in 1935 and 12,000 in 1936. The service ceased with the outbreak of World War II and was resumed after the war. During the 1950s, "Husking Bee" trains to Kent,

Connecticut, offered New Yorkers a Saturday outing in the country during October. In addition, the Berkshire Line followed the Housatonic River for 75 miles between New Milford and Pittsfield. Like the Berkshire Mountain region, this area was popular among visitors from New York City.

The New Haven operated many other recreational excursions on the Berkshire.

During the summer months many New Yorkers rode the train to Lenox, Massachusetts, to hear a concert of the Boston Symphony at its summer home at Tanglewood, and then returned home on the evening train. In the summer, several trains had extra cars to bring young New York City and Fairfield County campers to and from the many summer camps located in the Berkshires.

The large B&A station in Pittsfield marked the end of the Berkshire Line. In 1947, I-2 No. 1304 will soon haul this train south toward New York. *Kent Cochrane. Thomas J. McNamara Collection*

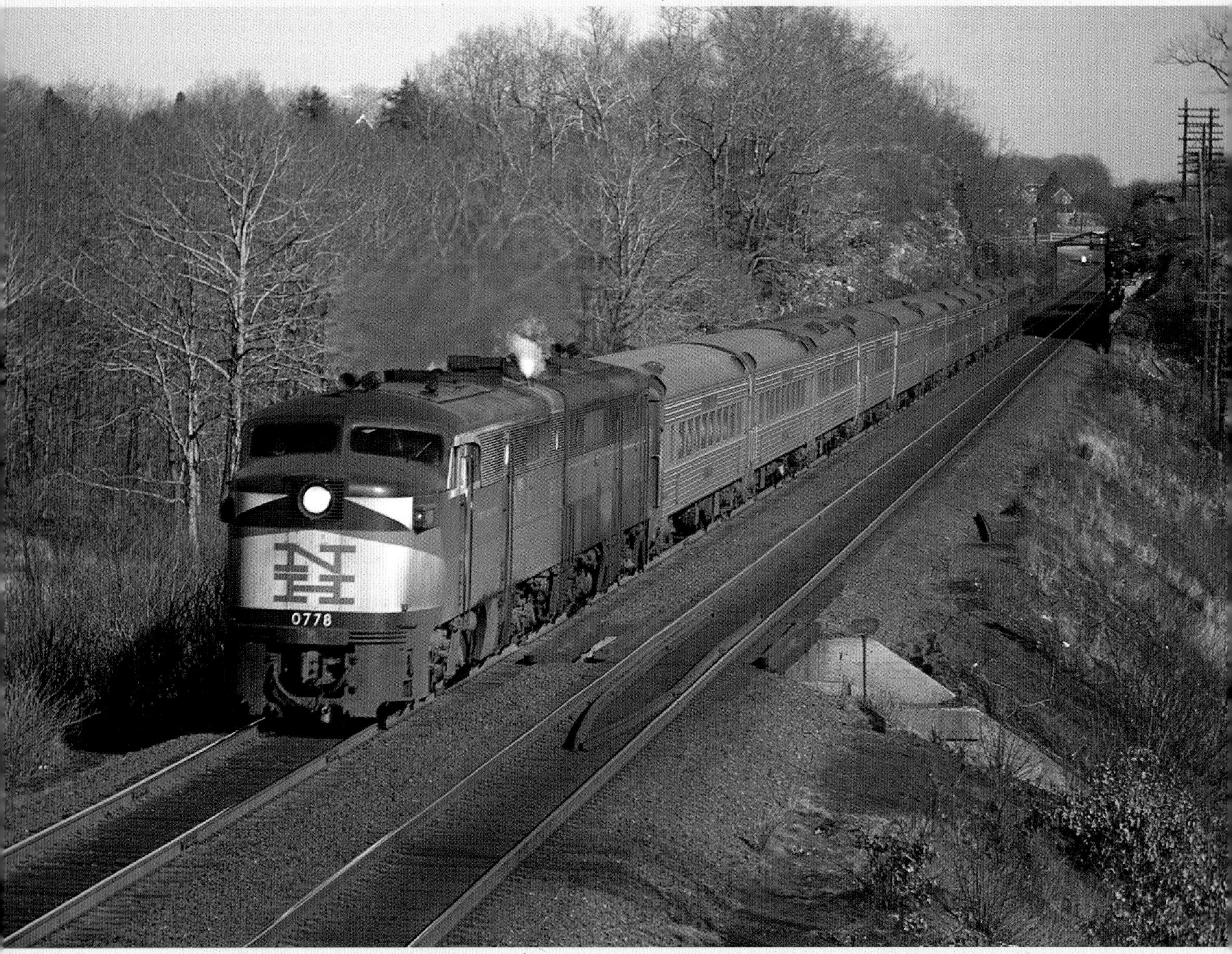
0778

CHAPTER SIX

PROVIDENCE DIVISION

The Shore Line

Under the control of the Providence Division were 143 miles of the New York-Boston route extending from Shore Line Junction, just east of New Haven, to Readville Transfer, a point 10 miles west of Boston, where the freight trains left the mainline for the Dorchester Branch. The Shore Line was a busy passenger and freight route; 79 miles per hour for passenger trains increased to 90 miles per hour east of Providence in 1956 and to 50 miles per hour for freight. Its double-track line increased to three or

Westbound *Yankee Clipper* rushes through Pine Orchard, Connecticut, in 1959. The lead PA unit has the McGinnis paint scheme. *Thomas J. McNamara* four tracks in numerous locations so that freight trains could be cleared to prevent passenger train delay. Because it closely followed the Connecticut coastline along the north shore of Long Island Sound for about 50 miles, the Shore Line was one of the most scenic in the nation.

Boston–New York trains made few stops along the Shore Line, but nearly all stopped in New London, Connecticut, where the New Haven shared the station and had an interchange with the Central Vermont Railway, which operated passenger trains until 1947. About half of the trains stopped at Old Saybrook, Connecticut, and Westerly and Kingston in Rhode Island. Although these communities were not large, all three served a number of other nearby towns with many residents who made frequent trips to Boston or New York. In 1953 a new station was added 12 miles west of Boston at an exit of the Route 128 highway, the first "beltway" in the nation to circle a major city. The Route 128 Station made it possible for many in the suburbs to get a train to New York without going into downtown Boston. All trains stopped at Route 128, and its huge parking facility also attracted many commuters to Boston.

The most important city served along the Shore Line was Providence, which, for many

Train No. 177, the *Senator,* races west by Shore Line Junction, the east entrance to Cedar Hill Yard, in 1956 with Pennsylvania Railroad *Congressional* equipment. *Peter McLachlan*

years was the largest city in the nation served by just one railroad. From a point just west of the station the double-track mainline widened to four tracks that extended six miles to Boston Switch, the junction with the line to Worcester.

Providence had a large station with seven through-platform tracks, plus additional stub tracks. The electric service to Bristol and Fall River had its own tracks at the eastern end of the station complex. There were four freight-yards near the station, one on each side of the mainline at both ends of the station. Just east of Providence Station was the Charles Street engine house with 50 tracks and two round-houses, each with a turntable. Further east, the two eastbound main tracks were separated from the two westbound by the two-mile-

long Northup Avenue hump yard. At one time Providence had more than 200 weekday commuter trains, and in the early years of the twentieth century the station regularly handled 30,000 passengers per day and often more. In addition to trains on the mainline, in the 1920s Providence had commuter trains to and from Worcester and New Bedford in Massachusetts and Washington and Pascoag in Rhode Island, as well as half-hour electric service to Bristol, Rhode Island, and Fall River, Massachusetts. The depression brought an end to all branchline service except that to Worcester and the electric service between Providence and Bristol, both of which were sharply curtailed.

The Shore Line was the route of the New Haven's premier trains, which operated every

Saturday local train No. 400 heads east through East Haven in 1957. This little train was following the *Yankee Clipper* and would make nine stops on its 50-mile run from New Haven to New London. *Thomas J. McNamara*

85

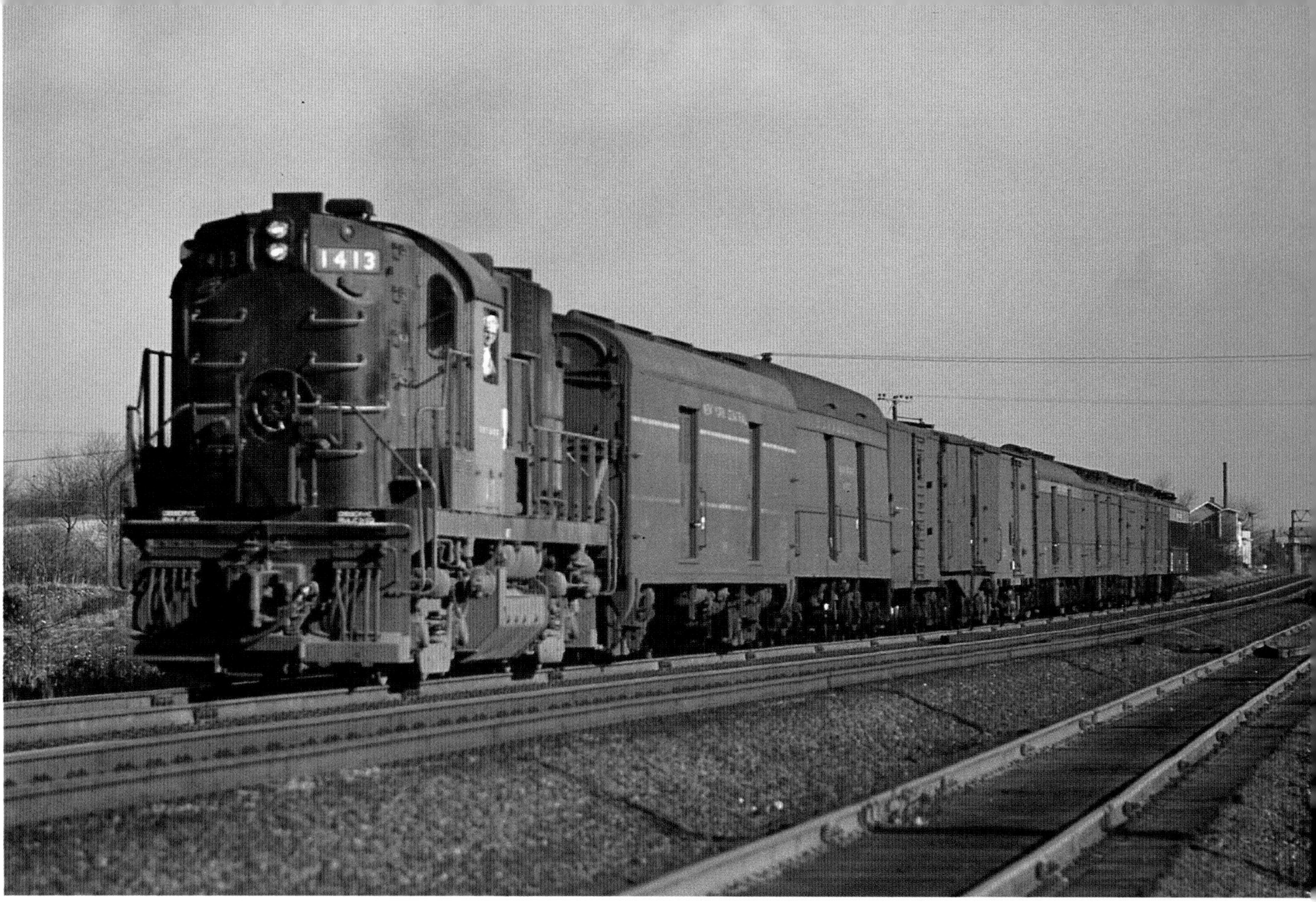
1413

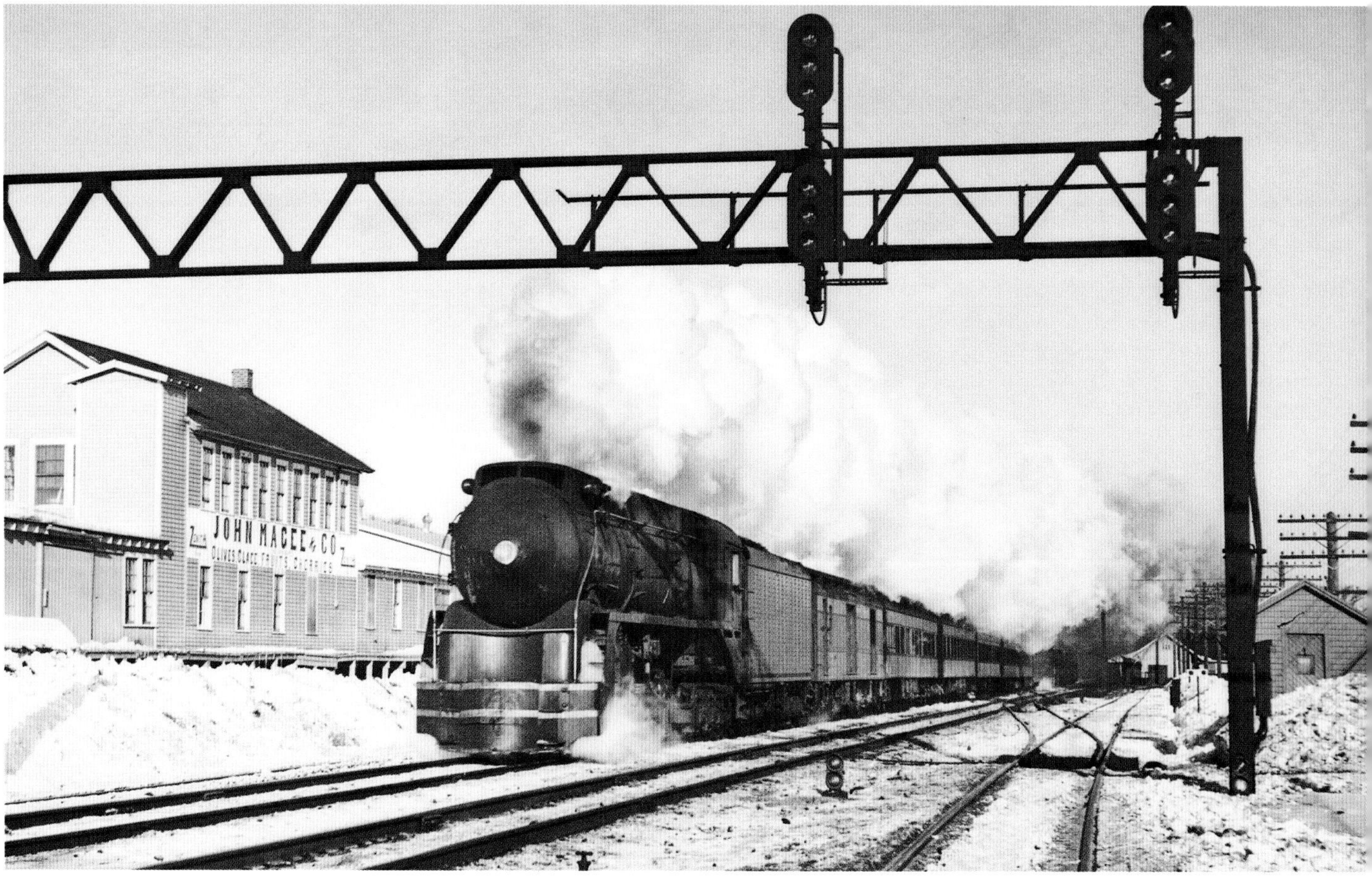
JOHN MAGEE & CO

hour in each direction all day long between Boston and New York, with some continuing on the Pennsylvania Railroad to Washington. The two most prestigious were the *Yankee Clipper* and the *Merchants Limited*. The *Yankee Clipper* left Boston and Grand Central Terminal at 1 P.M. and the *Merchants* left at 5 P.M. Both trains had parlor cars with spacious reclining single seats, dining cars, and, in later years, coaches. They made stops only at Providence, New London, and New Haven, completing the run in four hours.

Travel was so heavy that during the 1950s the New Haven also operated the *Advance Merchants Limited*, which departed New York City and Boston at 4:45 P.M. Some of the many other name trains on this route in and out of Grand Central included the *Mayflower*,

Above: Train No. 13, the *42nd Street,* approaches the station at East Lyme and Niantic, Connecticut, in June 1965. Just right of the train and out of frame is the beach bordering Niantic Bay. The location was halfway between Grand Central and Boston. *David W. Jacobs*

Opposite, top: The New Haven was a large carrier of U.S. mail, some on regular passenger trains, much more on dedicated mail and express runs that mostly ran at night. This extra was running west on the Shore Line though Old Saybrook, Connecticut, during the 1957 pre-Christmas season. *Thomas J. McNamara*

Opposite, bottom: In early 1948, an I-5 Hudson speeds the *Yankee Clipper* by Old Saybrook Station on its way to New York. *Kent Cochrane. Thomas J. McNamara Collection*

Above: Fairbanks-Morse road switcher 592 pulls a cut of cars west from the Central Vermont Railway interchange. The unit in a McGinnis paint scheme has just passed the station in New London. *Peter McLachlan*

Train No. 26, the *Merchants Limited,* heads east through Midway, Connecticut, under the coal tower in 1948. Shortly, the *Merchants* will have new PA diesels and stainless steel equipment. *Kent Cochrane. Thomas J. McNamara Collection*

Murray Hill, Bay State, Puritan, Gilt Edge, and, at night, the New York-Boston sleeping car train, the *Owl.* Three day trains in each direction went to Washington via Penn Station: the *Senator, Colonial,* and *Patriot,* plus the *Federal* at night. During the day, the *William Penn* and, at night, the *Quaker* ran between Boston and Philadelphia. An overnight train between Grand Central and Portland, Maine, the *State of Maine,* operated on the Shore Line to Groton, and after 1946, to Providence, to reach the Boston & Maine Railroad in Worcester.

During the daytime there was a fast passenger train in each direction every hour on the Shore Line, with occasional through and local freights mixed in. New London had local commuter trains to New Haven and Providence in the morning, with each returning in the evening. In addition, a dozen local trains ran in each direction between Providence and Boston to handle commuters from stations along the line. At night the operation changed dramatically. Several trains with sleeping cars ran on the route, and considerable mail and express traffic moved on several trains, some of which hauled no passengers. In fact, freight operation on the Shore Line was heaviest at night.

Passenger service increased in the summer months when both day and night trains from New York City to points on Cape Cod and Maine were added. There were also additional summer weekend trains between

Saturday afternoon train No. 525 from Providence heads west through Stonington, Connecticut, bound for New London in 1947. This train, with its baggage car and Railway Post Office, was a large mail and express hauler. The I-4 Pacific 1361, once on premier trains between New Haven and Boston, is now relegated to local service. *Kent Cochrane. Thomas J. McNamara Collection*

Providence and New York City, the *Seashore* and the *Cabana*, to handle passengers from seaside points along the Shore Line.

During World War II the volume of traffic on the Shore Line was overwhelming. In addition to regular passenger and freight trains, the New Haven ran extensive troop trains for soldiers headed abroad, as well as those on furlough. Several extra trains were devoted to war cargo routed through the various ports served by the New Haven. In contrast to World War I, the Shore Line, with its vastly improved signal system and sufficient motive power to move both passenger and freight trains at high speed, operated well during World War II. Even with postwar reductions in traffic through the late 1950s, there were still 35 to 40 trains in each direction on the Shore Line, with even more east of Providence. This was a fast and busy railroad, operated by people who knew how to move a high volume of passengers and

freight at high speed. Before Interstate 95 and air shuttles, the Shore Line was *the* conduit for both passengers and freight between New York City, Providence, and Boston.

Despite many hurricanes and "Nor'easters," the Shore Line, because it was solidly built in spots right along the water's edge, seldom had weather-related problems. However, this was not the case in 1938 when a massive hurricane charged up the Connecticut River. A book the New Haven Railroad published for its employees in October 1938 states:

"On September 21, 1938, with flood waters already threatening major washouts at important points....suddenly, just before dark, in the teeth of a howling southwest gale which increased momentarily into hurricane proportions, a steadily rising tide which in some places rose twenty feet in as many minutes, swept inland along the New England coast line....carrying on its crest hundreds of boats, ships, cottages, buildings and wreckage."

In 1958 a Boston-bound train with Fairbanks-Morse "C" Liner 798 in the lead heads east through Wickford Junction, Rhode Island. On this 10-mile-long, three-track section, passenger and freight trains could be separated using the middle track with signals in both directions. *Thomas J. McNamara*

The New Haven had more than 100 washouts with virtually every line affected. A total of 75 miles of track, 31 bridges, and 200 culverts were destroyed. The most serious damage was along the Shore Line for 35 miles between Saybrook and Stonington, where extensive, long washouts required rebuilding of the entire, double-track right-of-way in several locations.

On that afternoon, train No. 14, the *Bostonian*, had stopped for a red signal at Stonington with the train's last few cars still

Headed to Boston in 1954, an eastbound Shore Line express leaves Providence Station with the Rhode Island state capitol in the background. The cars still have the pre-McGinnis green trim around the windows. *Thomas J. McNamara*

on the causeway along the harbor when a tidal wave washed out the roadbed. The three rear cars were turned on their sides, but miraculously all but two of the passengers waded or swam to safety. The New Haven mobilized 5,000 people working around the clock, and in 13 days the Shore Line was reopened for normal business. As a result of the hurricane, all of the New Haven damaged trackage was restored. The passenger service to Bristol, already downgraded from electric to gas-electric operation, was a casualty of the storm and was not restored even though the trackage was. To keep freight moving while the Shore Line was out of service, the Air Line route via Middletown and Willimantic was used to move eastbound freight from Cedar Hill to all points east. In the 15 days between September

24 and October 8, 133 freight trains ran east on the Air Line.

Two Routes to Worcester

Worcester, Massachusetts, was a significant junction that provided the New Haven with a connection to eastern Massachusetts, New Hampshire, and, most importantly, to Maine, a large source of passenger and freight traffic. Worcester was a large source of freight traffic because of the many industries located there.

The New Haven had two routes in and out of the city. The primary route was the former Norwich & Worcester Railroad (N&W), a 70-mile single-track line that connected to the Shore Line just east of New London at Groton, Connecticut. The line north of Groton was familiarly known on the

New Haven as the Norwich Branch and followed the Thames River for 14 miles north to the port city of Norwich, Connecticut, where it passed through the middle of the U.S. Navy Submarine Base. In Norwich the track snaked beneath the city through two tunnels. Just north of the city the line shared its right-of-way with another New Haven subsidiary, the Connecticut Company, a carrier that operated electric trolley service over a 16-mile segment of the branch from the north end of Norwich through Jewett City and Plainfield to Central Village. In the early 1920s the trolleys made eight trips in each direction, but the service ended in 1926. At Plainfield the former Hartford, Providence & Fishkill line from Willimantic to Providence crossed the Norwich Branch at grade.

An important junction on the Norwich Branch was Putnam, Connecticut, 45 miles north of Groton. At an ornate masonry station, the former NY&NE line from Hartford and Willimantic joined the Norwich Branch to make it a double-track line for a mile and a half to Klondike, where the Midland Line separated to the east, heading for Boston. Alongside this double-track section was Putnam's fairly sizeable freightyard, used to transfer cars between trains of the two lines and to handle local industry. Just north of Putnam the line crossed into Massachusetts, passing through Webster and Auburn to reach Worcester.

Over the years, the Norwich Branch served a number of functions. In its earliest years it connected Worcester with a port and

Charles Street Engine House, the large locomotive facility in Providence, is shown during wartime. Another roundhouse was off to the left. This facility serviced the power for local passenger trains, through and local freights, and many yard crews. *J. W. Swanberg Collection*

This New York-Boston train with I-5 1403 has just passed the Sharon Heights tower, signal station 171, which controlled the east end of a third main track from Mansfield, Massachusetts. The third main was used for slower freights climbing Sharon Hill. Outside of the electric territory, the New Haven had left-handed semaphores that were larger, higher, and silhouetted against the sky, making them easier to see. *Kent Cochrane. Thomas J. McNamara Collection*

featured both passenger and freight boat trains. The most important function of the Norwich Branch, however, was as a freight route connecting with the Boston & Maine at South Worcester Yard and providing fast freight service to points in Maine. As for passenger service, the line had local service with two trains each way between New London and Worcester, plus two commuter trains from Norwich to New London, all of which—like the Connecticut Company's trolley service—lasted only until 1926. The nightly New York-Portland passenger train, the *State of Maine*, used the Norwich Branch until 1946, when it was diverted via Providence. In the summertime, especially prior to World War II, the Norwich branch had numerous sleeper trains from Washington and New York to Maine. The premier train, the *Bar Harbor Express*, ran in several sections, one right behind the other. To accommodate this traffic, the New Haven stationed operators every few miles along the line to space the trains.

A Boston–Providence local hauled by two PAs in 1958 slows for a stop at Sharon, Massachusetts.
With the discontinuance of some Shore Line trains earlier in 1958, some PAs were now hauling locals.
Thomas J. McNamara

The elaborate Putnam, Connecticut, Station seen in a pre-World War I postcard, was opened in 1907 after an eight-year battle between the railroad and the town, which said it needed a more suitable station to serve its growing population. From here a person could catch a train to New York, Boston, Hartford, New London, Worcester, or Maine.

N. Y., N. H. & H. R. R. Station,
Putnam, Conn.

A new Budd rail diesel car (RDC) waits to depart from the B&A station in Worcester, Massachusetts. This picture was taken in October 1952, four months after the restoration of local passenger service on this line to New London and 25 years after it had been discontinued. *Bob Liljestrand Collection*

After 25 years without local passenger service, the New Haven resumed Worcester-New London service in June 1952. This service, operated with a Budd RDC, initially ran three roundtrips per day that were cut to two in 1954. A convenient connection was provided to and from New York at New London: in the morning with the *Mayflower* and in the evening with the *Merchants Limited.* This service survived until the first day of Amtrak in 1971.

The other route to Worcester ran south through Rhode Island and joined the Shore Line at Boston Switch, five miles east of Providence. This route, owned by the Providence & Worcester Railroad and leased by the New Haven, was double-track until 1952. The largest town on the line was Woonsocket, Rhode Island. In 1920 the line had 10 roundtrip commuter locals between Worcester and Providence. By 1932 they were cut to four and by 1935 there was only one. In 1946 the *State of Maine* was rerouted via this line, allowing it to stop in Providence and also reducing interference with freight operations on the Norwich Branch. The *Bar Harbor* also used this route during the summer months. Until the end of the New Haven, there was a nightly freight from Providence to Worcester and back, moving Providence-area traffic to and from B&A and B&M interchanges, plus cars for the Woonsocket yard switcher.

The Providence–Worcester line was the home of an odd curiosity. In 1951 the New Haven acquired a railbus built by the Mack Company in Allentown, Pennsylvania. The new administration with Frederick "Buck" Dumaine, Jr. at the helm thought that this piece of equipment would be the answer to some of the lower-density branch and feeder

Just north of Putnam Station, R-1 3339 heads west by signal station 227. Headed toward Willimantic in the late 1920s, this is probably Boston-Hartford train BA-1, due in Putnam at midday. *J. W. Swanberg Collection*

lines, especially during off-peak, non-commuter hours. The railbus and RDCs increased Providence-Worcester local service in 1953 and 1954 to four roundtrips. The schedules made it possible for business travelers between Hartford and Providence to make a convenient morning and evening connection at Blackstone between Boston-Hartford trains.

Buck Dumaine had grand plans for nine more of these vehicles, which arrived in 1954, but by then the New Haven's new president, Patrick B. McGinnis, had declared that no more would enter regular service. A lone unit would make the single roundtrip between Worcester and Providence through 1956, when the service was cut back to operate only in Rhode Island for six months until discontinuance in 1957. The Mack railbuses outlived the New Haven, however: two were sold to the Sperry rail testing service, two to an industry in Bridgeport, and six to Spain.

Connecting to the Providence–Worcester line at Valley Falls, Rhode Island, just a mile north of the junction with the Shore Line,

was the Darlington Branch, a part of the circle route around Providence that served considerable heavy industry. This line joined the Bristol Line in East Providence, making it possible to return to Providence Station via the East Side Tunnel or head south toward Warren and Bristol. Also connecting in East Providence was the line known as the East Junction Branch that connected to the mainline west of Attleboro, Massachusetts. This line was the original route of the Boston & Providence and would have been the mainline if a dispute with the city of Pawtucket had not been resolved before World War I.

Located on the East Junction Branch was the Narragansett Park racetrack. Although not shown in the regular passenger timetables, the track had one or two daily trains from Boston every race day until the end of the New Haven. The "race trains," using commuter equipment during layover in Boston, left South Station in the late morning and returned from Narragansett after the last race, arriving back in Boston for the equipment to

The *Little Shoreliner*, a Mack railbus, makes its journey along the line between Providence and Worcester in Blackstone, Masschusetts, in 1956. This was the only line on which this equipment saw regular revenue service. Because the railbus was so light, it did not activate all crossing or signal circuits. *Thomas J. McNamara*

be used for evening rush hour. On some Saturdays a Budd RDC would come from Providence to the racetrack. The Budd car made a connection from an eastbound Shore Line train at Providence Station in the morning and made a return connection in the evening. Excursion tickets to Narragansett were regularly sold from points along the Shore Line. The service did not require much advertising because racing fans knew when the trains ran.

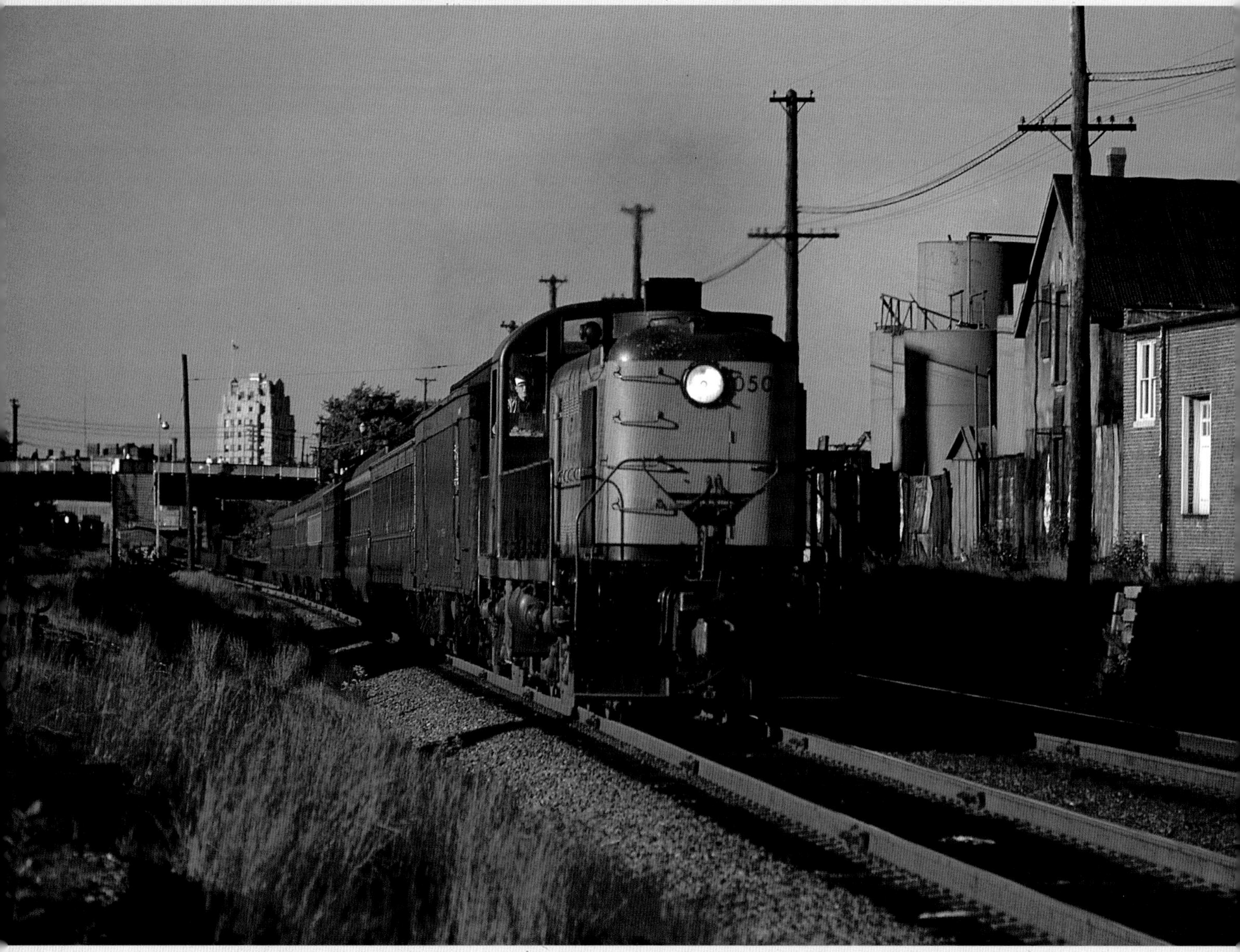

CHAPTER SEVEN

BOSTON DIVISION

Boston and the Old Colony

The focal point of the New Haven's Boston Division was South Station on Atlantic Avenue and Summer Street in downtown Boston. This semicircular structure was one of the largest stations in the nation. It was owned by the Boston Terminal Company, a jointly owned company, 80 percent by the New Haven and 20 percent by the Boston & Albany (a subsidiary of the New York Central Railroad). Opened in 1899 with 23 platform tracks, South Station would be the busiest rail station in the United

Heading south through Quincy on the double-track portion of the Old Colony between Boston and Braintree in 1957 is an RS-3-hauled local. *Thomas J. McNamara*

States until shortly after the 1913 opening of the new Grand Central Terminal in New York. South Station also had an unused lower level with loop tracks intended for suburban electric multiple-unit service that never began. A huge train shed spanned the station tracks and two five-story wings, which for many years were filled with operating, engineering and administrative offices of both railroads, fanned out from the station. With the New Haven divided into Lines East and Lines West until 1927, South Station was the headquarters for its eastern half.

What made South Station so busy in the early years of the twentieth century was the New Haven's extremely intricate Boston commuter network. In 1920 the New Haven had over 400 trains every weekday in and out of South Station. In addition to New York and Washington service, South Station ran commuter trains to 27 destinations. Half of the trains used the Shore Line via Back Bay, Boston's second station, which was slightly over a mile west of South Station. All of these trains stopped at Back Bay, convenient to many offices and theaters and other cultural venues.

Heading west off the Shore Line were two lines of the former New York & New England. At Forest Hills, trains left the mainline for Needham, Massachusetts, plus Woonsocket and Pascoag in Rhode Island. At Readville, trains diverged onto the Midland Line for Franklin and Blackstone in Massachusetts, and Willimantic and Hartford in Connecticut. Between these two routes was the "Dedham Loop," a double-track line parallel to the mainline that diverged from the

The *Yankee Clipper* leaves South Station in Boston during the summer of 1948. Still hauled by steam, the *Clipper* now has new stainless steel equipment. *Kent Cochrane. Thomas J. McNamara Collection*

Needham Branch and reconnected to the mainline at Readville so that a train could head back to Boston. Until the 1930s the New Haven had loop trains that left Boston both via the mainline or the Needham Branch and made an 18-mile circle, returning to Boston on the other line. Also, the Midland had the Dorchester Branch, another line into South Station that bypassed Back Bay with local commuter trains as far as Readville, plus some local trains that continued west onto the Midland route.

Heading south from South Station was the Old Colony route, with numerous tributary lines fanning out all over southeastern Massachusetts. The first five miles of the route had four main tracks that narrowed to double-track at Atlantic, Massachusetts, where a five-mile bypass via West Quincy to Braintree began. In 1920, about 30 of the 180 weekday trains on the Old Colony used the West Quincy Branch. A short branch to Mattapan that split off just south of Boston became part of the Boston Transit system in 1927.

At Braintree, two important commuter branches headed southeast to Greenbush and Plymouth. These two lines connected at Kingston, providing two routes to Plymouth. Continuing due south of Braintree was the route to Cape Cod via Middleborough that split at Buzzards Bay for Woods Hole and Hyannis/Provincetown. At Woods Hole and Hyannis, trains connected to steamers bound for Nantucket and Martha's Vineyard. Trains could leave the Cape Cod route at Braintree Highlands, using the old Dighton & Somerset route to Taunton, or proceed west from Boston on the Shore Line and return to the Old Colony, either at Canton Junction or Mansfield, providing three routes to reach either New Bedford or Fall River. All three routes had regular service in the 1920s, with some Fall River trains operating further south to Newport, Rhode Island. Until 1937 the *Fall River Line Boat Train* left Boston every evening for the Fall River Wharf, where passengers could board the overnight steamboat to Fulton Street in New York City. In the

Back Bay Station, next to Copley Square and a mile west of South Station is shown in 1929. It was just reopened, having been rebuilt after fire destroyed it. *Bob Liljestrand Collection*

A 1957 Providence-bound local heads west from Canton Junction with a pair of RDCs. *Thomas J. McNamara*

In the fall of 1952, local No. 523, pulled by a DL-109, heads west through Readville for Providence. The two tracks in the foreground are the Dedham Branch and the Midland to Blackstone, Putnam, and Hartford. Shortly, this train will pass underneath the bridge carrying the Midland track east into Boston via the "Second District," the freight-only Dorchester Branch to Boston. After the train passes under the bridge, Readville freight yard will be on its left. *Arthur E. Mitchell*

morning the train returned to Boston after the arrival of the boat from New York.

Boston-area commuter service sharply contrasted with the New York service, which was neatly concentrated on a single mainline with two feeder lines. The Boston lines, especially those in the Old Colony system, ran all over southeastern Massachusetts in a complex and involved spider web pattern. This service would plague the New Haven's management and finances for many years. Between the early-1920s and the time of the New Haven's bankruptcy in 1935, Old Colony service lost half of its riders. The 1920s were extremely hard on branchline operations all over the country. The automobile, along

An Old Colony local train just out of South Station in 1957.
Thomas J. McNamara

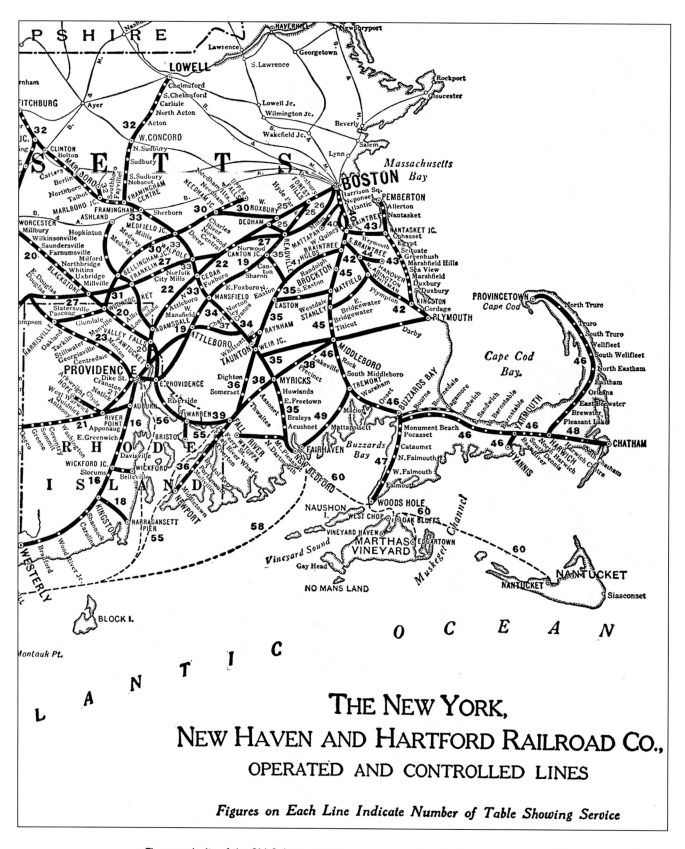

The complexity of the Old Colony commuter network south of Boston is depicted on this map from a New Haven Lines East timetable dated July 21, 1924. The number on each line refers to the table number where schedules for that line were shown in this timetable.

with improved bus service, drained many passengers from already lightly patronized rail lines. The depression years further accelerated this decline. As the New Haven's trustees worked to reorganize the railroad's finances after 1935, immense effort was put forth to deal with the Old Colony, which at the time was still a separate company. The New Haven let it go bankrupt, but the courts did not relieve the New Haven from operating the property. The New Haven put forth several plans to either turn the operation over to the state or curtail or restructure services, but was thwarted for several years by Massachusetts state agencies and courts. By 1937, the New Haven was operating more than 200 daily commuter trains in the Boston area on 300 route miles with steadily declining passenger use. By contrast, in the New York area, the

New Haven had 124 trains on only 104 route miles with increasing ridership. By 1940, the New Haven managed to cut the number of Old Colony trains in half and reduce the route miles by a third. Considerable overlapping service was discontinued and many off-peak trains were eliminated.

As World War II turned the New Haven's attention to other matters, the Old Colony settled down. After the war the New Haven continued efforts to reorganize and in October 1947 emerged from bankruptcy. Because the bankruptcy settlement provided that if, after October 1949, the service lost more than $500,000 per year, it could be discontinued, Old Colony service would live under threat of discontinuance ever after. In 1948, Old Colony finances again made the Boston papers as the New Haven made

In 1948 this southbound Old Colony train stops at Atlantic, 5 ½ miles south of South Station. The signals to the left protect the switches that bring the railroad from four-track to double-track. *Kent Cochrane. Thomas J. McNamara Collection*

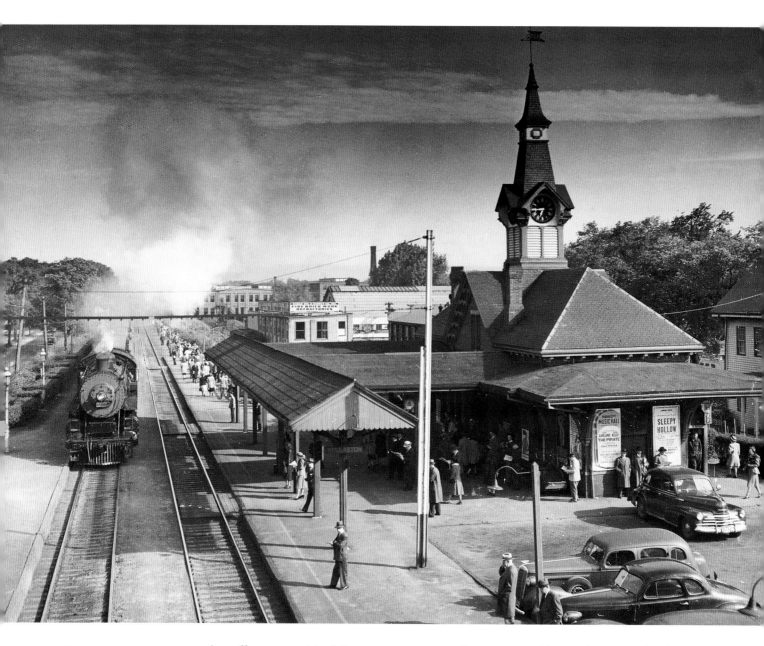

A Boston-Braintree local slows for a stop in Wollaston in 1947 with an I-2 Pacific. The reason that the commuters on the platform are not rushing toward this train is that they await a northbound that will arrive shortly after the southbound departs. *Kent Cochrane. Thomas J. McNamara Collection*

another effort to get rid of the service completely. For its part, the New Haven was accused of assigning excessive costs to the Old Colony, which always had the oldest New Haven equipment; in fact, it was the last area of the New Haven where steam was used. However, the Old Colony network was different than other New Haven routes because it had no through-passenger or freight traffic and there was little freight-generating industry in many of its locations. After months of very public battle, more curtailments were made. By 1949 all that remained were four morning and evening rush hour trains on each of the routes from

Boston to Plymouth, Greenbush, and Middleborough, with two trains continuing to Buzzards Bay to split for Hyannis and Woods Hole. The Canton Junction Line was downgraded to a shuttle to North Easton, connecting to Boston–Providence local trains at Canton Junction. New Bedford service via Mansfield was cut to two trains in each direction. Fall River lost all service, giving it the distinction of being the largest city in the United States with no rail passenger service.

The Cape and the Colony

Summer service to Cape Cod had a long history. The post-Civil War period saw the Cape,

along with Martha's Vineyard and Nantucket, become summer resorts. The Old Colony would provide service to accommodate this growth, and in 1884 the exclusive *Dude Train* was established to provide a fast escape for Bostonians going to Martha's Vineyard and returning during the summer months. The train was a subscription-only train with Pullman as well as private cars. The *Dude* lasted until the onset of World War I.

Because travel to the Cape was very heavy, summer months on the southern portion of the Old Colony were financially beneficial. For three or four months each year it was a strong route because riders from Boston and New York rode a much longer distance on Cape trains than on other branches. After World War II, the New Haven restored Cape Cod service from New York with more train service than ever. From June through September, the *Day Cape Codder* operated daily between New York and Hyannis, split-

ting at Buzzards Bay for Woods Hole. The *Night Cape Codder* left New York City on Friday nights for Hyannis and Woods Hole and returned Sunday evening. The most popular Cape Cod train, however, was the *Neptune*, which left New York on Friday evening and returned Sunday night, and which for many years operated with 12 or more cars. In 1949, despite the sharp cutbacks in Old Colony service, the New Haven established the summer-only *Cranberry*, a weekday express that left Boston in the late afternoon and returned from Woods Hole and Hyannis in the morning. Buzzards Bay, where all trains either split into Hyannis and Woods Hole sections or joined together to head for Boston or New York, was a busy spot on the Old Colony. This location was unique in that the railroad actually came to town before the waterway: The drawbridge at Buzzards Bay, first opened in 1911 and then rebuilt at its present location in 1935, crossed the Cape

In 1948 a southbound approaches Braintree hauled by I-2 1302. The first two and the second rear coaches with the crescents above the windows were former New York, Boston & Westchester multiple-unit electric cars converted to coaches at Readville Shops. The track in the foreground is the West Quincy Branch, which was the Granite Railroad built in 1826, the oldest portion of the New Haven. *Kent Cochrane. Thomas J. McNamara Collection*

The *Day Cape Codder* from New York meets a steam-hauled excursion train at Tremont in the summer of 1948. In just over 10 minutes the *Cape Codder* will arrive at Buzzards Bay to split for Woods Hole and Hyannis. *Kent Cochrane. Thomas J. McNamara Collection*

DL-109 No. 722 was painted red to haul the *Cranberry*, a summer-only express between Boston and Cape Cod that started running in 1949. This 1953 postcard shows the locomotive on an excursion run, accounting for the white flags designating it as an extra train.

Cod Canal created and operated by the U.S. Army Corps of Engineers.

In the early-1950s passenger service on the Old Colony and other New Haven branchlines saw some renewal. Buck Dumaine, who took over as the New Haven's president in 1951, believed in right-of-way maintenance and saw an opportunity to increase the number of passengers in several areas. This effort was assisted by the acquisition of 40 Budd RDCs starting in 1952. These cars offered an opportunity to offer more economical service, especially when operated singly, requiring just a two-person crew. They could also quickly reverse direction without the need to be turned. The RDCs began to arrive on the New Haven in 1952 and were used on numerous Old Colony trains. As a result of Buck Dumaine's expansion, the Old Colony lines, which offered a total of 19 roundtrips in 1951, had 52 roundtrips by 1953. Off-peak service was once again available, service on most lines was doubled, and Fall River service was reinstated. In 1954 a modern Centralized Traffic Control (CTC) signal system was also installed on the Cape Cod route between Braintree and Buzzards Bay and speed was increased to 79 miles per hour.

The Old Colony upswing lasted for a few more years until 1956, after which the New

I-2 1317 with the Woods Hole section waits at Buzzards Bay to join the Hyannis section for the run to Boston. The drawbridge in the background crosses the Cape Cod Canal and is operated and maintained by the U.S. Army Corps of Engineers. *Kent Cochrane. Thomas J. McNamara Collection*

111

The picturesque Old Colony depot in Taunton, Massachusetts, had the two main tracks passing through the station building. *Ben Perry, Jr.*

Haven once again started to incur deficits. The railroad's president at that time, George Alpert, began to make the case that if the public wanted commuter service, public funding was needed, and once again in 1958 the New Haven proposed to abandon all Old Colony service. The Commonwealth of Massachusetts came forward with a $900,000 subsidy for one year, which saved all service except trains to Fall River and New Bedford, which were cut back to Stoughton, just four miles off of the Shore Line, leaving 52 route miles without passenger service. The following year, Massachusetts decided not to renew the subsidy, and on June 30, 1959, all Old Colony service ended. The New Haven never again provided commuter service on the Old Colony except for summer service from New York to Hyannis and Woods Hole, which continued through 1964. A further deterrent to service restoration around Boston came in 1960, when the trestle carrying the double-track approach to the Neponset River drawbridge, just south of the city, was badly damaged by fire. The entire Old Colony network would complete its life under the New Haven solely as a network of local freight branchlines.

Commuter lines on the west side of the Shore Line fared better than the Old Colony. Service on the Blackstone route was increased in 1954 and remained at seven roundtrips, even after service between Boston and Hartford was discontinued in 1955. The Needham Branch also continued to have considerable service under the New Haven, with 11 daily roundtrips, including one rush hour trip further west of Needham to West Medway. Providence-Boston service continued throughout the New Haven years with nine weekday roundtrips.

North of the mainline from Mansfield was the line to Framingham, which split in that city and continued to Lowell and Fitchburg. But because Framingham was reached more quickly by the Boston & Albany commuter trains, and points along the Fitchburg and Lowell lines were served by faster trains in and out of the B&M North Station in Boston, these northern Old Colony lines became freight-only in the early-1930s. These lines served some local industry but their primary purpose to the New Haven was for freight interchange with the Boston & Albany at Framingham and with the Boston & Maine at various points along the lines to Fitchburg and Lowell.

DL-109 0702 heads for Boston in 1958 on the Needham Branch which joined the mainline at Forest Hills, five miles west of South Station. *Thomas J. McNamara*

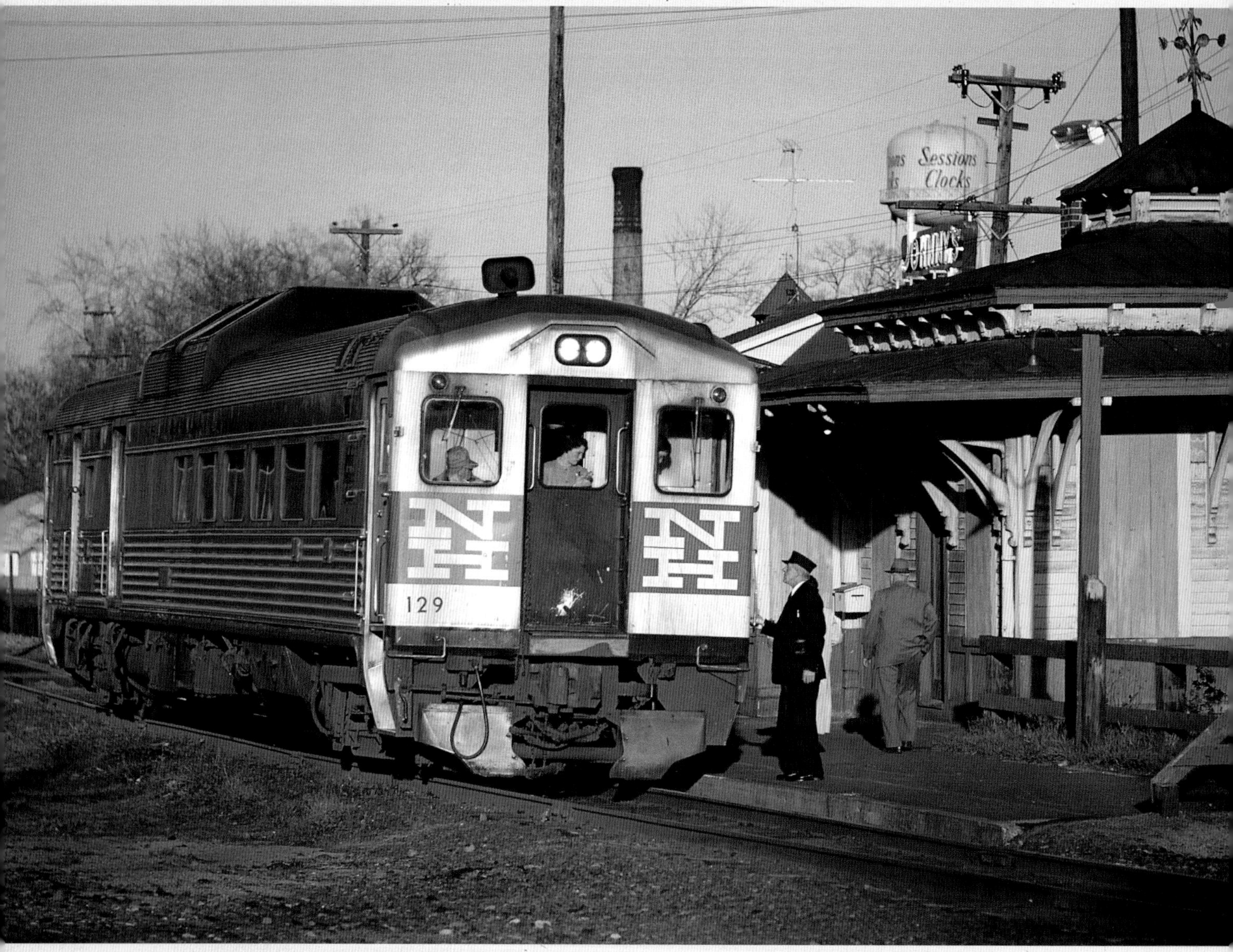
Sessions
Clocks
129

CHAPTER EIGHT

HARTFORD DIVISION

The Hartford-Springfield Line

For the first 20 years of the New York, New Haven & Hartford Railroad, the New Haven-Hartford-Springfield line was the Consolidated's mainline. Once the Shore Line came under New Haven control, it became the New Haven's main route to Boston. However the "Hartford," as it was known on the New Haven, remained the important second mainline. This route, all 60 miles of it double-track since 1872, was a 70-mile-per-hour passenger and 50-mile-per-hour freight railroad.

A single Budd car stops at Forestville, Connecticut, on the way to Hartford in 1958. This single RDC commuter roundtrip between Waterbury and Hartford would last another two years. *Thomas J. McNamara*

Passing Air Line Junction S.S. 80 is a northbound headed for Springfield in 1956 with DL-109 0721. The first two tracks are the Hartford Line, the adjacent tracks lead into Cedar Hill Yard, and the far tracks on top of the wall are the Shore Line tracks to Boston. *Peter McLachlan*

The Hartford separates from the Shore Line at Mill River Junction, 2 miles east of New Haven Station, and then turns sharply north. For more than 5 miles it runs along Cedar Hill Yard to North Haven. It does not follow the water until Windsor Locks, Connecticut, where it crosses the Connecticut River at Warehouse Point and follows the east bank for the last 10 miles into Springfield, Massachusetts. This route is much different in appearance than the Shore Line because it passes through several heavily industrialized towns: North Haven, Wallingford, Meriden, Newington, and Windsor Locks. From Berlin, a short branch heads west to New Britain to connect to the Hartford-Waterbury line.

The most important point on this line was Connecticut's capital city, Hartford, with its spacious stone station. On the upper floors were the operating headquarters of the Hartford Division. For 5 miles south of Hartford, starting at Newington, were four

main tracks, two being the Hartford-Springfield line and the other two the Waterbury line. Numerous adjacent industries lined both sides of this four-track railroad. North of Hartford Station were two single-track Albany Avenue tunnels, just south of which the Waterbury tracks joined the Hartford tracks. Once north of the tunnel, the former New York & New England line diverged eastward, crossed the Connecticut River, and headed to Boston. This junction provided access to the south end of Hartford's freightyards, which paralleled the line to Springfield.

Twenty-five miles north of Hartford is Springfield, Massachusetts, where the New Haven connected with two railroads, the Boston & Maine and the Boston & Albany, the latter a subsidiary of the New York Central. All three railroads shared the B&A station. Coming north into Springfield, a New Haven train could veer sharply east into

Right: A northbound stops at the ornate Wallingford, Connecticut, depot in 1968. *George E. Ford*

Below: Heading for New Haven is an I-5 Hudson on a southbound Springfield-New York train just through Berlin, Connecticut, in 1946. The semaphore signal adjacent to the second car is just beginning to drop from clear to stop and proceed. *Sturman F. Dyson, Jr. Thomas J. McNamara Collection*

Stopping at Berlin, Connecticut, in 1955 is a southbound extra flying white flags. *Thomas J. McNamara*

A northbound freight approaches Newington Junction, Connecticut, in 1947. This train will drop cars in Hartford and then terminate in Springfield. *Kent Cochrane. Thomas J. McNamara Collection*

the passenger station headed toward Boston or head straight north, crossing the B&A mainline to the B&M line. Trains pulled into Springfield unless destined for the north, in which case they ran north of the diamond and then backed into Springfield Station.

Passenger service was frequent on the Hartford. Until the late-1950s when there was some curtailment, there was hourly service from early morning until late evening and some service at night. The *Bankers* and the *Nathan Hale* provided fast morning service from Hartford line points to New York, operating non-stop from New Haven. These trains carried parlor and dining cars as well as coaches, and returned in the evening as the *Connecticut Yankee* and the *Nathan Hale*. Until late 1966, this line featured the daily, overnight sleeper train between Washington and Montreal via Penn Station. The *Montrealer* northbound and the *Washingtonian* southbound operated to the Boston & Maine

at Springfield and then further north on the Central Vermont and Canadian National. All other Hartford trains operated to Grand Central with many connecting to or from Shore Line trains. This allowed passengers a quicker trip between New Haven and New York if they transferred at New Haven to or from faster Shore Line trains that made only one or two stops west of New Haven. Service on this line was programmed to offer hourly morning and evening rush-hour commuter service in and out of New Haven, as well as for Hartford both from the north and south. A single train could provide commuter service into three cities: Hartford, New Haven, and New York.

The Hartford was also the connection from New York City to central Massachusetts, Vermont, and New Hampshire. In addition to the night Montreal train, the New Haven operated the *Ambassador*, a day train between Grand Central and Montreal that served

The northbound *Ambassador* pulled by two FL-9s slows to stop at Hartford in 1963 on its way north to Springfield and Montreal. *Bob Liljestrand Collection*

119

Train No. 136, with I-2 1320 from Waterbury, leaves Hartford for Boston in 1947. Shortly, it will diverge from the Hartford Line and head east toward Willimantic. *Kent Cochrane. Thomas J. McNamara Collection*

Holyoke, Northampton, and Greenfield in Massachusetts and numerous points in Vermont. Until the late-1950s half of the Hartford Line trains had connections to Boston & Maine trains running at least as far as Greenfield, with some as far as White River Junction, Vermont. In conjunction with the B&M, the New Haven also operated summer trains, such as the *North Wind* and the *Night White Mountains*, to the northern New Hampshire towns of Woodsville, Littleton, and Bretton Woods-Fabyan. In the 1920s this was a regular "Presidential" route when President Calvin Coolidge journeyed from Washington to his home in Northampton,

Massachusetts, or to his family farm in Vermont. The Hartford Line was also an "education corridor." On weekends and school holidays, regular trains and sometimes extra trains were jammed with students from New York and Connecticut returning to the many prep schools and colleges all along the route. Some New Haven trains had cars that went beyond Springfield to Boston via the B&A, offering service through New Haven to Worcester, Framingham, and Wellesley. After 1952, changing trains in Springfield was required.

The Hartford was the first New Haven line to receive extensive weekend excursion

service. On Sundays in the 1930s the New Haven had a surplus of passenger equipment on hand in New Haven, laying over until Monday morning commuter runs. At this time reduced commuter service operated on Saturday mornings, returning from New York between noon and 2 P.M. To utilize this idle equipment, starting in 1936, the New Haven ran three pairs of excursion trains on Sundays: New York to Springfield, Springfield to New York, and Hartford to New York. Special tickets, with the roundtrip price being close to the weekday one-way fare, were good only for one day on the designated excursion train. The Hartford Line would also, for many years, offer numerous special trains to New York City for baseball games, the World's Fair, the New York Flower Show, the Bronx Zoo, and other events. Also in 1936, the year after it started ski trains on the Berkshire Line, the New Haven began running ski trains to Vermont; they left New York on Friday night

with sleepers for points along the B&M, and returned Sunday evening.

During the 1950s three or four through-freight trains ran per day in each direction between New Haven and Springfield, and two each way in the 1960s. Much of the freight on this line ran at night when passenger trains were less frequent. There was only one interlocking tower along the Hartford line, in the city of Hartford. Getting passenger trains around slower freight was cumbersome and further complicated by many highway crossings throughout the line. The train crew had to operate switches by hand if they were required to run by train order on the opposing track. The usual operating practice required that a freight train have sufficient time to get to Hartford ahead of a passenger train before being released from Springfield or Cedar Hill Yard at North Haven. At Berlin, Connecticut, 25 miles north of New Haven, the "Canal" trains

A northbound train for Springfield is crossing the Connecticut River Bridge between Windsor Locks and Thompsonville, Connecticut, at Warehouse Point. The second diesel, the 0759, was the only one of the 60 DL-109s to receive the McGinnis paint scheme. *Thomas J. McNamara*

121

Train No. 77 leaves the B&A station in Springfield for New York in July 1968, just months before the Penn Central took over the New Haven. On an adjacent track, a Penn Central freight heads for Boston *George E. Ford*

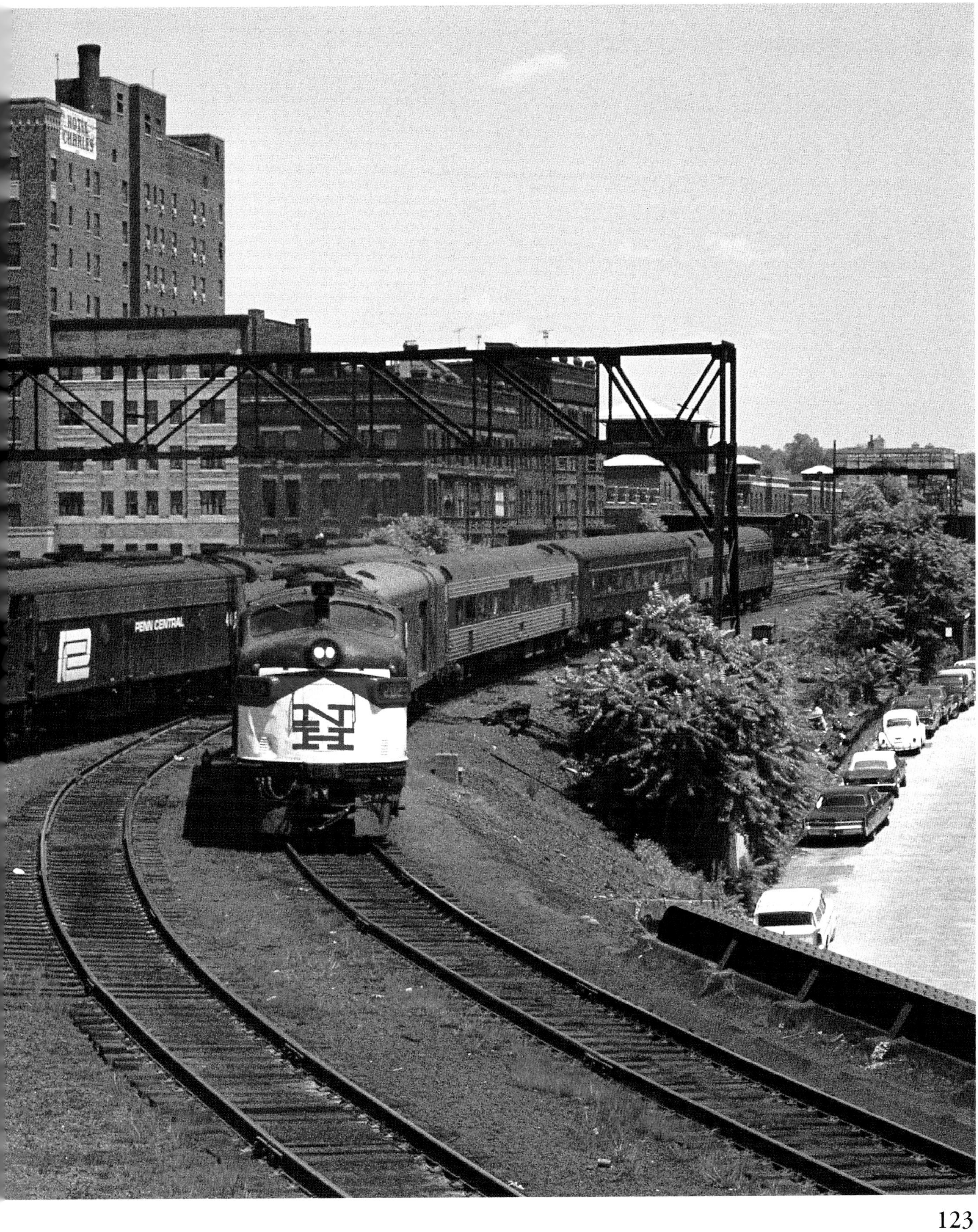
HOTEL
CHARLES
PENN CENTRAL

Left: Train No. 130 heads east toward Boston through the crossing switches at Bridge Street in Willimantic, Connecticut, in 1953. The diagonal black target on top indicates that the switches were lined for the Hartford–Boston route. *Arthur E. Mitchell*

Below: The rest of the story is that the smoke behind train No. 130 was not from its RS-3 but a Central Vermont freight waiting to head south to New London. Once the operator lines the switches, the CV train will see the black target swing to vertical position. *Arthur E. Mitchell*

from New Haven branched off to go west to New Britain and Plainville and then north to Westfield and Holyoke, Massachusetts.

The High, Dry & Dusty

Also part of the Hartford Division was the former New York & New England line from Hartford to Boston. The "High, Dry & Dusty," so named because it did not follow the coastline or any river and—once a few miles east of Hartford—it operated mostly through sparsely populated, remote areas, was once the mainline between New York and Boston. It was busier in the last years of the nineteenth century than it ever would be again. Once the Shore Line route was under New Haven control, service on the former NY&NE line diminished. Until the depression, there would be a train known as the *Highland* each way from Boston to New York, but with basic

passenger service operated between Boston and Hartford with three trains per day each way, two of which went on to Waterbury. Until the depression there was also a morning commuter train from Willimantic to Hartford that returned in the evening.

New Haven trains shared eight miles of the double-track on the High, Dry & Dusty between East Hartford and Vernon with the hourly electric trolley service of the Connecticut Company, a New Haven subsidiary, from early morning until late evening. At Vernon these trains branched off onto a short New Haven branch extending to Rockville, 4-1/2 miles north of Vernon. The electric service lasted until 1925 when it was replaced by limited Rockville–Hartford steam service, which continued until 1928.

The 57 miles of the line as far as Putnam belonged to the Hartford Division. More

Just west of Putnam, Connecticut, the north- and southbound *East Wind* between New York and Portland, Maine, meet each other as directed by a timetable at the siding at Hampton, Connecticut, in 1954. *Thomas J. McNamara*

125

This "Ford Train" hauling automobile cars for Readville will reach the "High, Dry & Dusty" in about two hours. In 1963 this train was on the Maybrook Line headed east through Hawleyville, Connecticut. The three perishable cars on the head end are probably destined for Hartford. *Thomas J. McNamara*

than half of this route was double-track in the early twentieth century, but by 1936 it was all single-track except for 2 miles at East Hartford. The line also had a good deal of straight track and much of it was authorized for 55 miles per hour. In Willimantic, the line crossed the Central Vermont Railway (which ran south from the Canadian border to New London), the Air Line to New Haven, and the old Hartford, Providence & Fishkill line east to Providence. This junction, at which all four lines joined and then separated just west of the Willimantic passenger station, was protected by antiquated signals with lanterns hung on each end of two rectangular targets.

Switches were lined by hand and then targets were adjusted to display the appropriate signal for the desired route. This operation—known as "Bridge Street" for the crossing that the operator also protected—continued until 1961.

Service on the High, Dry & Dusty continued until the late summer of 1955, when interior Connecticut experienced severe flooding. A bridge just west of Putnam was damaged and never replaced, ending the Boston–Hartford–Waterbury passenger service, with only local freight service operating west of the commuter station at Blackstone, Massachusetts. One exception was the use of

Left: I-1 Pacific 1031 built in 1910 is on the mainline with a Waterbury train in Stratford, Connecticut, in 1947. In a couple of minutes this train will leave the mainline and head north through Devon up the "Naugy." *Kent Cochrane. Thomas J. McNamara Collection*

Below: Train No. 131 from Boston to Waterbury is west of New Britain, Connecticut, in 1951. *Thomas J. McNamara*

the line as the New Haven's "*O-D*" (Over-Dimension) route. Freight cars that were too high to fit under the catenary or bridges along the Shore Line moved on special trains from Maybrook through Waterbury and Hartford via the High, Dry & Dusty to Boston. After the bridge washed out in Putnam, cars moved eastward on the Providence Line from Willimantic to Plainfield and then north on the Norwich Branch to continue east from Putnam. During the 1960s the New Haven had a once-per-week move of automobile-carrying cars known as the "Ford Train" proceeding from Maybrook to an auto-unloading site in the Readville Shop complex.

Waterbury: The Naugy and the Highland

In 1930 the Waterbury Division, which consisted of the double-track "Naugy" (Naugatuck) from Devon (the junction with the mainline) to Waterbury and became a single-track branch north from Waterbury to Winsted,

was merged into the Hartford Division. East of Waterbury, the double-track "Highland" ran east to Hartford. These lines passed through a heavily industrialized area of Connecticut: Waterbury was known as the nation's "Brass Capital," Kerite produced underwater cable in Seymour, Naugatuck had U.S. Rubber Company, Derby and Ansonia had steel mills, and Thomaston was home of Seth Thomas, the clockmaker that not only produced decorative small timepieces but also billboard-sized clocks.

Frequent passenger service was provided between Waterbury and Bridgeport; and connections with trains to or from New York City were made at Bridgeport. Some trains operated north of Waterbury to Winsted or east on the "Highland" to Hartford. Until the flood of 1955, which brought havoc to all three of these lines, a through-train, the Naugatuck, operated south from Winsted to New York in the morning and returned in the evening.

The Highland featured trains that operated between Bridgeport and Hartford via Waterbury, commuter trains between Waterbury and Hartford, and two trains per day in each direction between Waterbury and Boston via Hartford. In the 1930s continuing through 1948 the Highland also had Sunday excursion trains to and from New York via Waterbury. While some Waterbury services to Bridgeport and Hartford were commuter trains, this was essentially branch-line passenger service that dwindled in the 1950s. By 1960 all of it was single-track, with the only remaining passenger service a single RDC (occasionally two RDCs) making four daily roundtrips between Waterbury and Bridgeport. Because of local industries, however, freight operations in the Waterbury area continued to produce a considerable volume of traffic through the end of the New Haven.

At the north end of the Naugy in Winsted, Connecticut, trains from Waterbury used the CNE tracks and station. This RDC was in Winsted on an excursion in 1954, when two passenger trains per day still ran in and out of the town. *Arthur E. Mitchell*

129

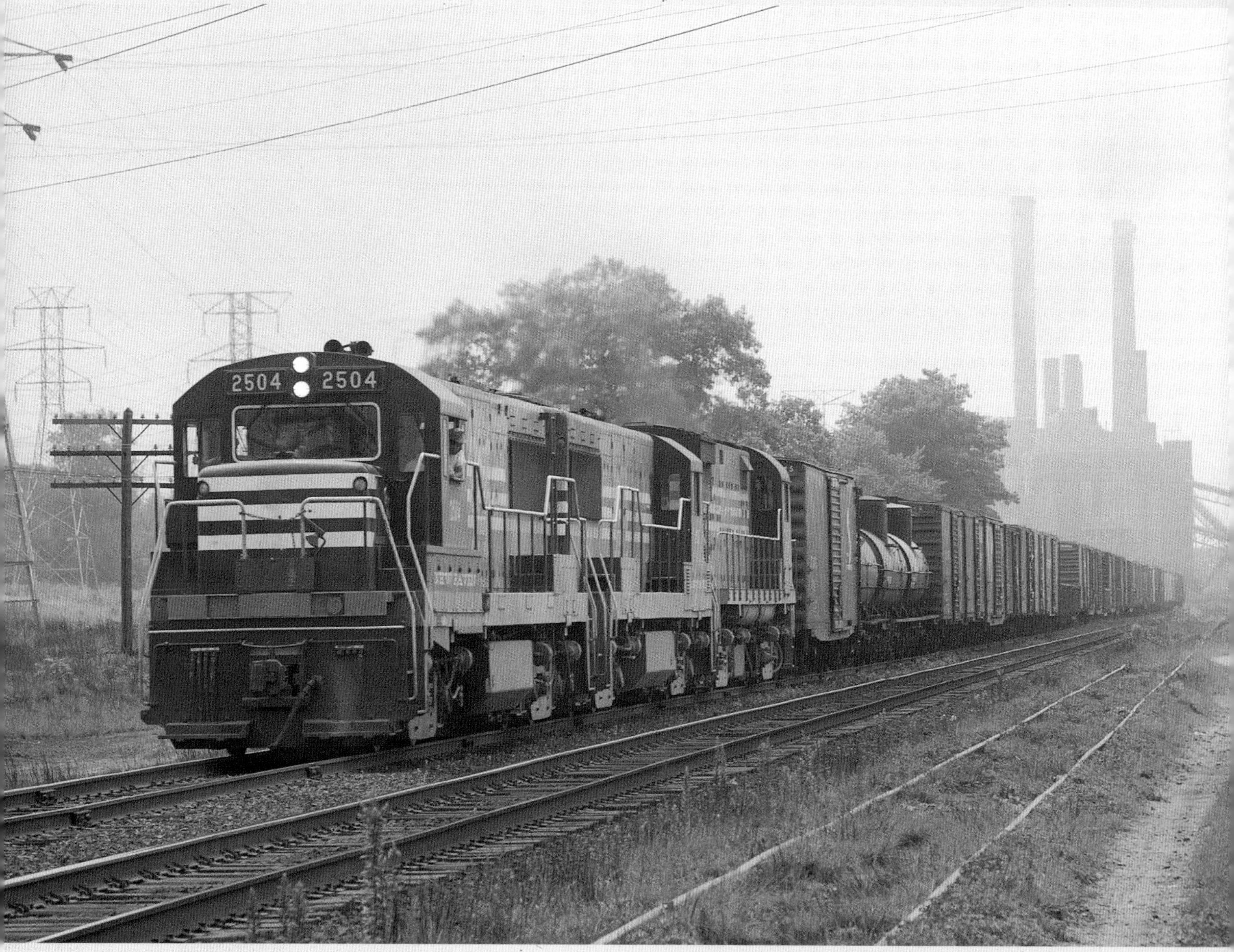
2504
2504
NEW HAVEN

CHAPTER NINE

FREIGHT OPERATIONS

W hile generally known as a passenger railroad, the New Haven's freight operations were substantial. In fact, after 1912 freight revenues always exceeded passenger revenues. Some statistics are available to describe the complexity of these freight operations. In 1953, for example, the New Haven had 82 daily scheduled freight trains that operated at least five—and often seven—days a week. There were more than 200 switching crews working out of 32 switching yards every day and 59 local-freight crews that

In 1965 a westbound Maybrook freight heads north on the eight miles of the "Naugy" shared by Waterbury and Maybrook trains between Devon and Derby Junction. *Thomas J. McNamara*

131

worked six days per week out of 29 different locations. That same year, the New Haven interchanged freight cars with 23 other railroads at 39 different locations. It was often said that the New Haven was just a large freight terminal. Its longest freight haul was from Maybrook to Boston, a distance of 275 miles, making for very intense freight activity in a small area. For decades the New Haven brought in most of the food, raw materials, and finished goods needed in southern New England. And it shipped out many of the products that the region once manufactured.

The New Haven directly served many industries and operated huge terminals and freight houses in major cities such as New York, Bridgeport, New Haven, Providence, Hartford, and especially Boston. The railroad's April 1936 *Arranged Freight Train Service* booklet reads: "At Boston the New Haven Railroad has one of the largest terminals in the United States with 12 freight houses containing more than 300,000 sq. ft. of floor space and tracks for placing 600 cars; also bulk tracks for loading and unloading 1350 cars daily." In addition, at the Boston Market Terminal "25,000 carloads of fruits and veg-

etables are received and distributed annually along with three separate large pier facilities for rail-water transfer of cargo." The various railroad-owned freighthouse facilities were served by another New Haven subsidiary, New England Transportation Company, a motor carrier whose trucks picked up and delivered freight moved over the New Haven.

The basic pattern of freight movement on the New Haven was straightforward. Although the railroad had numerous connections to the west, there were three major "service" connections to and from western connections via Chicago, St. Louis, and Cincinnati: the Pennsylvania Railroad via the Bay Ridge–Greenville car floats across the Hudson River; the Erie Railroad via the Maybrook interchange; and, also via Maybrook, Central States Dispatch, also known as the "CSD" or the "Alphabet" route. A car routed from Chicago, St. Louis, or Cincinnati on the CSD moved in an expedited manner over seven railroads via the Baltimore & Ohio yard in Cumberland, Maryland, and Maybrook on the New Haven: the Western Maryland, the Reading, the Central Railroad of New Jersey (CNJ),

Marine operations. A New Haven tug pushes a car float into Oak Point in the mid-1950s. *Arthur E. Mitchell*

A Long Island Railroad crew at Bay Ridge puts a caboose on a New Haven freight in 1953. At Bay Ridge, LIRR crews did all the switching and float loading and unloading for the New Haven, using Pennsylvania Railroad "B-type" electric freight switchers. *Fielding L. Bowman*

The engine tracks and eastbound yard at Maybrook, New York, shown in 1951. *Bob's Photos. J. W. Swanberg Collection*

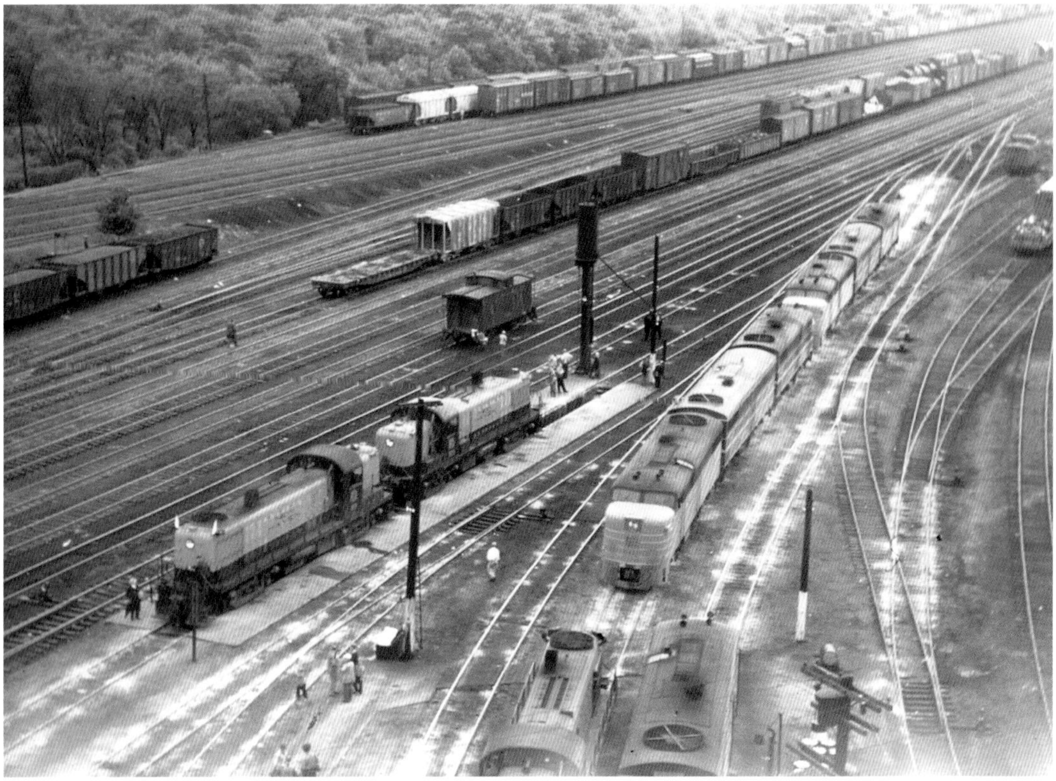

Below: Along Whaley Lake, Connecticut, four FA units pull a westbound toward Maybrook in 1953. *Thomas J. McNamara*

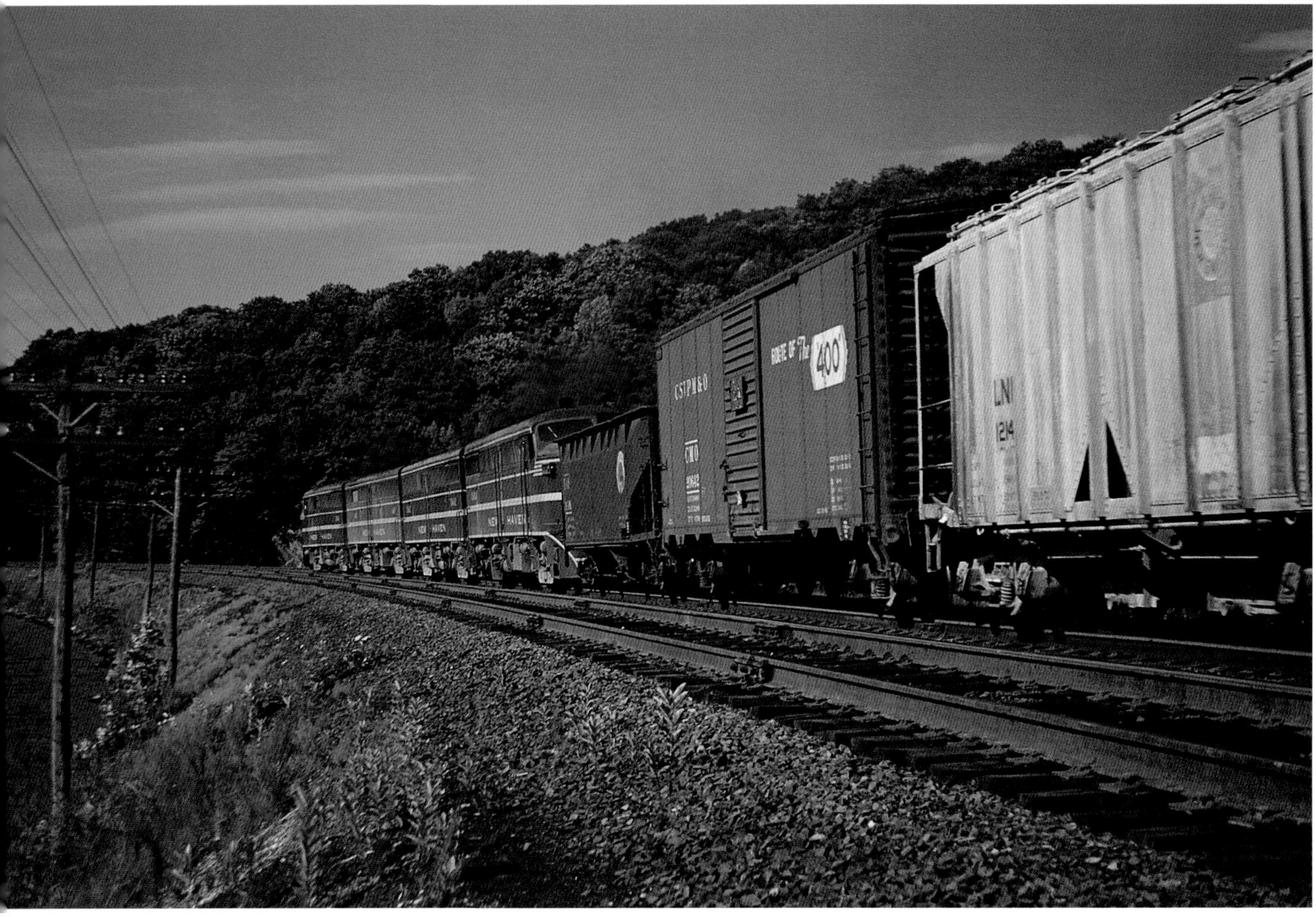
ROUTE OF The 400
CSTPM&O
CMO
LNI
1214
NEW HAVEN

the Lehigh & Hudson River, and New Haven. To connect from the CNJ and L&HR the train moved a short distance on a PRR branchline. A variation on this route replaced the B&O with the Nickel Plate Road, the Wheeling & Lake Erie, and the Pittsburgh & Lake Erie.

To and from southern points along the East Coast, the New Haven had two basic connections: the Pennsylvania via Bay Ridge car float or the B&O/CNJ via car float between Jersey City and Oak Point.

The New Haven's two primary connections via its Oak Point car float operations were with the Central Railroad of New Jersey and the Lehigh Valley, both of which provided the New Haven with considerable traffic from New Jersey and eastern Pennsylvania. Car floats also connected the New Haven with its Brooklyn terminals: Bush, Brooklyn Eastern District, and Jay Street. Located at Harlem River there was extensive lighterage (a barge operation that transferred cargo between railcars and ships). Eight miles west of Oak Point was Fresh Pond Junction, site of the New Haven's interchange with the Long Island Railroad.

At Maybrook and Campbell Hall the New Haven also connected with the New York, Ontario & Western, a partly New

A westbound Bay Ridge freight heads toward New Haven Station through the East Cut in 1965. *Thomas J. McNamara*

135

Cars rolling down the hump are classified in the East Class Yard at Cedar Hill in the late-1940s. The towers on the left and right control the switches and retarders that squeeze the wheels to slow the cars. Cars to the far left are in the Westbound Receiving Yard and will be classified on the West Hump facing the opposite direction. *J. W. Swanberg collection*

Haven-owned subsidiary that provided some traffic from western New York and the Scranton area. The New York Central's Catskill Mountain Branch provided some traffic from that railroad's West Shore route (the line south from Albany to northern New Jersey). Another important line that fed cars to the New Haven at Maybrook was the Lehigh & New England that served the cement producers in the area around Easton and Allentown, Pennsylvania.

On the New Haven, eastbound or inbound traffic consisted of almost all loaded cars. From Bay Ridge and Oak Point, trains went to Providence, Boston, and local points west of New Haven, with most cars going to Cedar Hill Yard for reclassification. Traffic

moved in a similar fashion from Maybrook, with one or two trains going on to Waterbury and Hartford until the early-1950s. At Cedar Hill, traffic from Maybrook and Bay Ridge was switched and consolidated for movement on road trains to points all over the system. Trains destined for Boston, Providence, the Central Vermont Railway at New London, Worcester, New Bedford, and South Braintree operated eastward on the Shore Line. Trains for Hartford, Springfield, and Holyoke ran north on the Hartford, and trains for Waterbury operated west from Cedar Hill to Devon and then northward on the Naugy.

Westbound traffic was handled in a slightly different manner. In the late after-noon or early evening, the New Haven had

Train AO-3 from Hartford to Maybrook heads west on the Highland toward Waterbury in 1952. *Thomas J. McNamara*

"closing times" all over the system for the acceptance of loaded freight cars, known on the New Haven as "hot" cars, for movement that same day. These cars were gathered at Boston, Readville, Providence, New London, Cedar Hill, and East Bridgeport for movement on expedited trains. The *Speed Witch* operated from Boston to Bay Ridge, sometimes in two sections, and provided overnight service via the floats to Philadelphia, Baltimore, and Potomac Yard, just south of Washington. The *Jet* from Boston to Maybrook provided expedited service to Maybrook for both the Erie and CSD routes. Westbound empty cars, of which the New Haven had many, were gathered at all points and sent to Cedar Hill for forwarding back to the owning railroad; loaded traffic was given priority over empty cars.

The piggyback business between Harlem River, Providence, and Boston started in 1938 and had grown so that by the early-1950s the

A Shore Line freight hauled by two PA units in 1958 passes Canton Junction, where the branch to Stoughton, Taunton, and New Bedford heads south. In half an hour, this train would be in Boston. *Thomas J. McNamara*

A short freight bound for Cedar Hill pulled by R-3a 3559 heads south on the Naugatuck Line through Beacon Falls, Connecticut, in 1948. Within two years the steam and the second track will disappear from this line. *Kent Cochrane. Thomas J. McNamara Collection*

New Haven had two piggyback trains in each direction between Harlem River and Boston. By the late 1950s the New Haven began to interchange piggyback cars for movement to and from the west. Primarily, this traffic moved via the Erie Railroad over the Maybrook interchange.

The Norwich Branch was the New Haven's important route to northeastern New England, primarily Maine. The New Haven operated high-priority, overnight service between Cedar Hill and Rigby Yard in Portland via Worcester and the Boston &

Maine on trains M-6 and M-7, known as the *Maine Bullet.* Especially important were the morning deliveries of newsprint and potatoes for Harlem River Yard in the Bronx. During the daytime an additional pair of trains ran on the Norwich Branch to handle more cars between Cedar Hill and the B&M points, as well as for industries along this line served by four local freights that worked the busy branch. At certain times of the year extra freight trains were made up solely of insulated cars of potatoes from Maine destined for Harlem River.

Running south on the Norwich Branch in 1968 is Train N-1 from South Worcester to Cedar Hill. N-1 is crossing the diamond in Plainfield, Connecticut, where the semaphore signals protect the crossing of the Providence-Willimantic line. *Thomas J. McNamara*

In eastern Massachusetts the New Haven had trains from Boston and Fall River to its interchanges with the New York Central's Boston & Albany Division at Framingham, and the Boston & Maine at Lowell. These interchanges primarily handled traffic for New Haven points on former Old Colony territory.

The New Haven had some unit train operations. Coal trains operated to two powerplants: one in Bridgeport, just west of the passenger station, and the other in Laurel, just south of Middletown on the Valley

139

Branch. Coal for both of these plants came to Maybrook from the L&HR and moved in unit trains directly to Bridgeport or to Cedar Hill, if destined for Laurel. For many years the New Haven also moved large blocks of oil in 20 or more tank cars north from New Haven to Holyoke or from East Providence to Worcester.

The dilemma of New Haven freight operations was the extent of its physical plant and its service and maintenance costs. In addition to the industries located on-line, many New Haven-owned freight loading and unloading facilities became increasingly expensive to operate with declining traffic and rising labor costs. In Boston, New Haven, Bridgeport, and Providence, industrial freight trackage ran through city streets, making the operation cumbersome and costly. Starting in the 1930s heavy industry began to leave New England, cutting outbound carloads so that many cars returned empty westbound. By the

In 1953 the New Haven joined with the Bangor & Aroostook to purchase these insulated State of Maine boxcars. There were 100 New Haven marked cars used to haul potatoes and other commodities from Maine to Harlem River. *Arthur E. Mitchell*

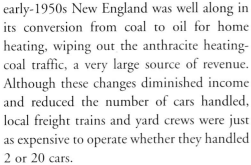

early-1950s New England was well along in its conversion from coal to oil for home heating, wiping out the anthracite heating-coal traffic, a very large source of revenue. Although these changes diminished income and reduced the number of cars handled, local freight trains and yard crews were just as expensive to operate whether they handled 2 or 20 cars.

A McGinnis-painted RS-3 hauls two cars on the Stepney Branch in 1956. This line was a piece of the original Housatonic Railroad in Connecticut that the New Haven served two or three times a week to deliver a couple of lumber, gas, or animal feed cars. Many such branchlines produced little traffic for the New Haven. *Peter McLachlan*

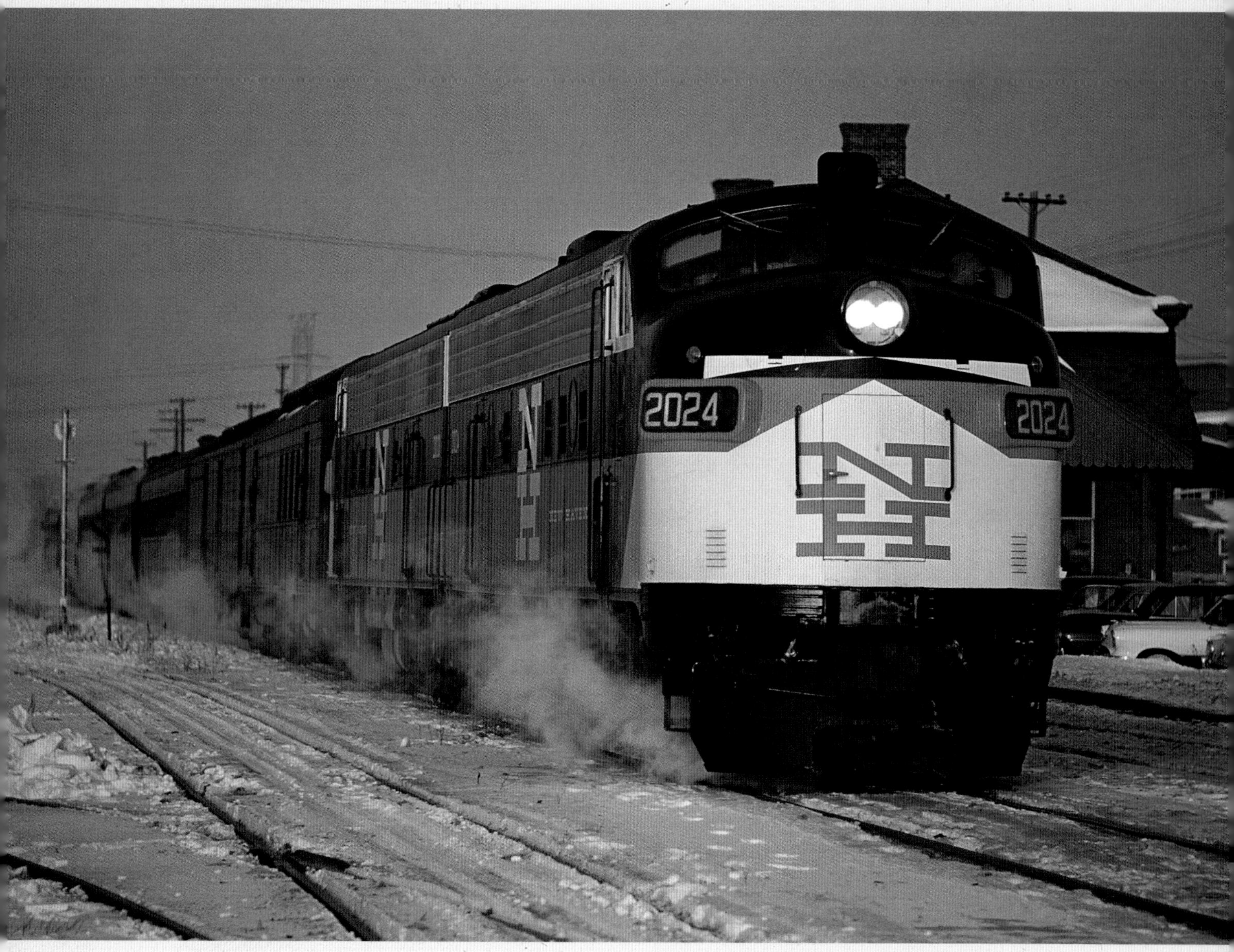
2024
2024

CHAPTER TEN

POSTWAR IMPROVEMENTS AND INEVITABLE DECLINE

1945–1968

The war years provided the New Haven with a great deal of revenue and left it financially strong. To match the new diesels ordered in 1946 and 1947 to eliminate steam power, 222 new stainless steel passenger cars, including coaches, parlor cars, sleepers, and dining cars, were ordered in 1946. These attractive silver cars with dark green trim around their windows arrived over the

A pair of new FL-9s, led by 2024, is stopped at Berlin, Connecticut, in January 1958. Train No. 71, a morning train from Springfield to Grand Central, was a large handler of U.S. Mail in its RPO. *Thomas J. McNamara*

Public timetable
from 1959
illustrates the
McGinnis logo.

course of several years and provided all regular Shore Line and some Springfield trains with new equipment. The New Haven also decided to buy some locomotives from a manufacturer other than Alco, ordering 10 "C Liner" (CPA24-5) road diesels and 10 H16-44 road switchers from Fairbanks-Morse between 1950 and 1952. The 2,400-horsepower road units were used on Shore Line and Springfield trains, while the road switchers were used, for a short time, on commuter runs and later on local freights.

After 12 years of bankruptcy, the New Haven was finally reorganized in September 1947. With a strong management team, new equipment, and a new office building to consolidate forces scattered around the railroad, financial prospects were bright. But more change was imminent. In May 1948, former New Haven director Frederick C. Dumaine, by that time 82 years old, got control of enough New Haven stock to control the board of directors and take the presidency away from Howard Palmer. Frederick C. promptly made changes, primarily cutting costs in order to increase dividend payments, some of which he personally received. His particular dislike was "high-paid" management, and he was reported to be after anyone making more than $10,000 per year. Beyond significant management reductions, other cuts Frederick C. made across the system included 20 percent of the New York-Boston trains. These reductions came with poor economic conditions in 1949 that saw revenue drop by 15 percent. The military buildup in Korea led to some economic recovery in 1950 and 1951, and the railroad, although it suffered some labor difficulties

THE NEW HAVEN RAILROAD

THE SCENIC SHORELINE ROUTE

SERVING NEW YORK AND NEW ENGLAND

EFFECTIVE JULY 26, 1959 ● DAYLIGHT SAVING TIME

brought on by operating and maintenance cuts, remained profitable.

Frederick C. Dumaine died in 1951 and was succeeded by his son, Frederick "Buck" Dumaine, Jr., who reversed some of his father's policies. He stepped up maintenance, stopped cutting service, and added trains all over the system. From 1951 to 1953, the New Haven became a highly regarded property.

While the RDCs were arriving on the east end of the system, 100 new stainless steel multiple-unit cars ordered for the Stamford-New York commuter service arrived in 1954. Also ordered in 1954 were 10 General Electric rectifier locomotives (EP-5s) that became known as "Jets" when they arrived in 1955.

The relative calm of the early 1950s was not to last. In 1953, Patrick B. McGinnis, a railroad stock speculator who had assisted the elder Dumaine in his 1948 takeover, had grown dissatisfied with the rate of payment of stock dividends in arrears and tried to take control of the New Haven but was thwarted. In 1954 another attempt succeeded thanks to a proxy battle promising to pay more dividends. Although his actual experience was limited to terms as president of two small railroads in the South, McGinnis viewed himself as a railroad innovator and visionary. His presence was quickly felt and he was fre-

quently known to say, "The railroad industry has been so devoid of thinking that everything you think about is new."

He decided to give the New Haven a new look and hired his wife, Lucille, to oversee this makeover. She in turn hired Herbert Matter of Knoll Associates, who produced a new logo, a modernistic block "NH," along with new equipment colors prominently featuring red-orange along with white and black. Many stations formerly decorated in dark green or brown were painted in every imaginable color. The new EP-5 electrics ordered by Buck Dumaine arrived with the bright new color scheme and logo.

Although McGinnis was ever-present on the railroad, he always had his eye on the dividends and cut maintenance severely to continue the payout to the shareholders. After two studies strongly recommending additional refurbishing of the Cos Cob powerplant

New RDCs run west on the Highland between Waterbury and Hartford in 1953. The train is nearing the approach signal for Plainville where the double track ended. *Thomas J. McNamara*

145

In July 1955 train No. 172, the *Federal*, was involved in a serious wreck in Bridgeport, Connecticut. The train left the tracks on 30-mile-per-hour Jenkins Curve while traveling at a speed estimated by the ICC to be 60 to 75 miles per hour. EP-4 363 lies upside down adjacent to Bridgeport Yard switcher 0949 and would not be restored to service. This photo was taken by Arthur E. Mitchell, who was the flagman on the wreck train. *Arthur E. Mitchell*

and the railroad's electric locomotives, the maintenance was slashed and, instead, large new orders for diesels were placed with General Motors in 1955 and 1956: 20 SW-1200 switchers, 30 GP-9 road switchers, and the first 30 of 60 FL-9 road diesels equipped to operate into Grand Central using third-rail shoes. Since GM had several large orders for GP-9s and could supply only 30 to the New Haven in 1956, the railroad also purchased 15 Alco (DL-701) and 15 Fairbanks-Morse (H16-44) road switchers. Around this time, McGinnis also had the idea of removing wire east of Stamford and converting all operations to diesel except for the Stamford-New York commuter trains.

Mismanagement Leads to Decline

The year 1955 began the New Haven's decline. Cuts in maintenance were accompanied by a huge public outcry about delayed trains and general mismanagement of the railroad. The situation was further aggravated by the wreck of the *Federal* in July 1955, when the overnight Washington–Boston train plunged over the bank on the curve west of Bridgeport Station and tied up the railroad for two days. The Connecticut floods of 1955 washed out a number of branchlines, most notably in the Waterbury and Putnam areas. Everything was rebuilt the following year except for a bridge between Putnam and Willimantic, ending service between Hartford and Boston.

McGinnis also decided to pioneer high-speed New York-to-Boston service and ordered three lightweight trains: the *Roger Williams*, a six-car modified RDC train; the *Daniel Webster*, a nine-car Pullman/Baldwin-Lima-Hamilton train; and the *John Quincy Adams*, a 15-car American Car & Foundry /Fairbanks-Morse train. The trains arrived in late 1956 and early 1957 equipped with third-rail shoes for operation into Grand Central. But the trains' sizes could not be adjusted; they did not have regular dining service; the ride was very rough, especially aboard the *Daniel Webster*, with its single set of wheels between each coach; and they proved unreliable and frequently caught fire

Rectifier electric 371 hauls a New Haven–New York local express west by the signal tower at Green's Farms, Connecticut, in 1958. *Thomas J. McNamara*

147

on the third rail. Within a year the only train operating was a part of the *Roger Williams*, used in Providence–Boston local commuter service. Neither the three trains nor the FL-9 diesels that did not need to be changed in New Haven could ever reliably match the performance or the time of a train hauled by an electric changing to or from a pair of PA diesels—the New Haven's New York–Boston service was vastly better in 1952 and 1953 than it was in 1955 and 1956.

By the spring of 1956 both the public and the railroad's board of directors had had enough of McGinnis, who departed to head the Boston & Maine, an assignment that would later land him in federal prison for accepting kickbacks on equipment and stations that the railroad sold. McGinnis was succeeded at the New Haven by another member of the board, Boston lawyer George Alpert, who was immediately faced with the challenge of acquiring enough cash to operate and maintain the railroad. While Alpert was able to secure some federal maintenance loans from the Interstate Commerce Commission for track work, the condition of the equipment

Left: Two DL-701s lead train No. 12, the *Bay State*, into Old Saybrook Station in 1957. Later that evening, when train No. 29, the *Gilt Edge*, stopped at Old Saybrook at 6:28 P.M., the postal clerk on the Rail Post Office (RPO) would get the mail from the box on the platform. A letter posted there would be delivered anywhere in the New York area the following morning. *Thomas J. McNamara*

was worsening and was later aggravated by the closing of the diesel shop at Readville and the electric shop at Van Nest in the Bronx. The shop facilities in New Haven could not keep up with the locomotive needs.

Casualty of Progress

A further blow came with the 1958 opening of the Connecticut Turnpike, later designated I-95. This road, built almost alongside the New Haven for miles, would seriously erode the railroad's Boston–New York traffic, which was further hurt by faster New York-Boston air service as jets took over. The result of the enhanced air and highway competition was a 25 percent curtailment of New York-Boston trains in 1958. In 1959 the Commonwealth of Massachusetts failed to continue the

The 1610, a new Fairbanks-Morse H-16-44, heads south on the Hartford Line at Newington, Connecticut, in 1957. *Thomas J. McNamara*

$900,000 subsidy for the Old Colony service, so that on June 30 the trains ceased running. This reduction in service, along with the arrival of the second 30 FL-9s in 1960, saw the DL-109s, many PAs, and all the electrics—both passenger and freight except the new "Jets"—end up on the growing dead line at Cedar Hill. The New Haven's neighbor to the north, the B&M, was having its own problems and in 1960 decided to quit running the *State of Maine* from Worcester to Portland. The New Haven rerouted the train to Boston.

As a result of the Old Colony situation, Alpert began to spend a good deal of time trying to persuade the public that private funding alone could not support rail commuter service. In the area of delivering a public mes-

sage, at least, the New Haven was once again an innovator. Despite Alpert's efforts, the New Haven could meet neither its debt obligations nor its payroll, and in July 1961 was again bankrupt. Three court-appointed trustees took over and kept the railroad afloat.

The operation of the railroad changed very little in the 1960s. All passenger service remained except for the weekday RDCs between Danbury and Pittsfield, which were discontinued in 1964. The Maybrook Line, converted from a double track to a single-track CTC west of Poughkeepsie in 1956, was made single-track all the way to Derby Junction in 1961, except for 5 miles through Danbury and three sidings. Branchline Abandonments—very minimal since the late-1930s—were resumed in the bankruptcy.

The 3101 pulls the *John Quincy Adams*, an American Car & Foundry/Fairbanks-Morse train, west through Wickford Junction, Rhode Island, in September 1957. *Thomas J. McNamara*

Between 1961 and the end of 1968, just over 200 route miles, more than 10 percent of the railroad's total mileage, was abandoned. These lines, with very little, or in some cases no traffic, had their track removed and the land sold.

The court-appointed trustees found that if the Cos Cob powerplant only produced peak power for the morning and evening commuter rush hours, supplemented by some commercial power, it was very expensive to operate. They calculated that it would actually be much more economical to use more power during non-commuter hours, especially if it could cut the cost of additional diesels hauling freight under the wire. First, they explored the restoration of wartime freight motors and discovered even after just a few years on the scrap line, they were so deteriorated that they would be too expensive to restore. Instead, they purchased a dozen 3,300-horsepower freight electrics—built in

1956 and 1957—from the Norfolk & Western, which had just removed the overhead wire from the recently acquired Virginian Railway. The locomotives arrived in 1964 and were hauling freight between Bay Ridge and Cedar Hill as soon as the overhead catenary was put back in service in Cedar Hill Yard and from Oak Point to Bay Ridge. The freight diesels also were in distress because of maintenance cutbacks so the trustees arranged to lease 25 GE U25Bs and 10 Alco C425s for the service from Cedar Hill to Maybrook, Boston, Springfield, and Worcester. The arrival of these new units in 1964 and 1965 spelled the end for the PAs—a few of which had been hauling freight—and most of the FAs. In 1965 and 1966 the New Haven relocated CNJ, LV and Brooklyn Terminal floating operations from Oak Point to Bay Ridge.

Now, the trustees had two key tasks: Find enough money to keep the New Haven in operation and devise a long-term solution.

The *Daniel Webster*, a Pullman-Baldwin Lima Hamilton train, heads east through Madison, Connecticut, in December 1957. *Thomas J. McNamara*

They proposed a reduction of service to Springfield and Boston and also the elimination of the New York commuter stops west of Larchmont to permit retirement of the older multiple-unit cars. In both cases, the states stepped in to provide stopgap funding. In Massachusetts, the Massachusetts Bay Transit Authority (MBTA) was formed after the Old Colony discontinuance, in the realization that other services could disappear, too. In 1966 MBTA provided commuter funding that also

cut service west of Franklin to Blackstone, west of Millis to West Medway, and the one remaining trip on the short Dedham Branch.

The trustees had to find a home for the New Haven, whose plant was becoming increasingly deteriorated without funds for needed repairs. As the extended talks about the proposed Pennsylvania and New York Central merger continued throughout the 1960s, the trustees concluded that inclusion in that system would be the only answer to

153

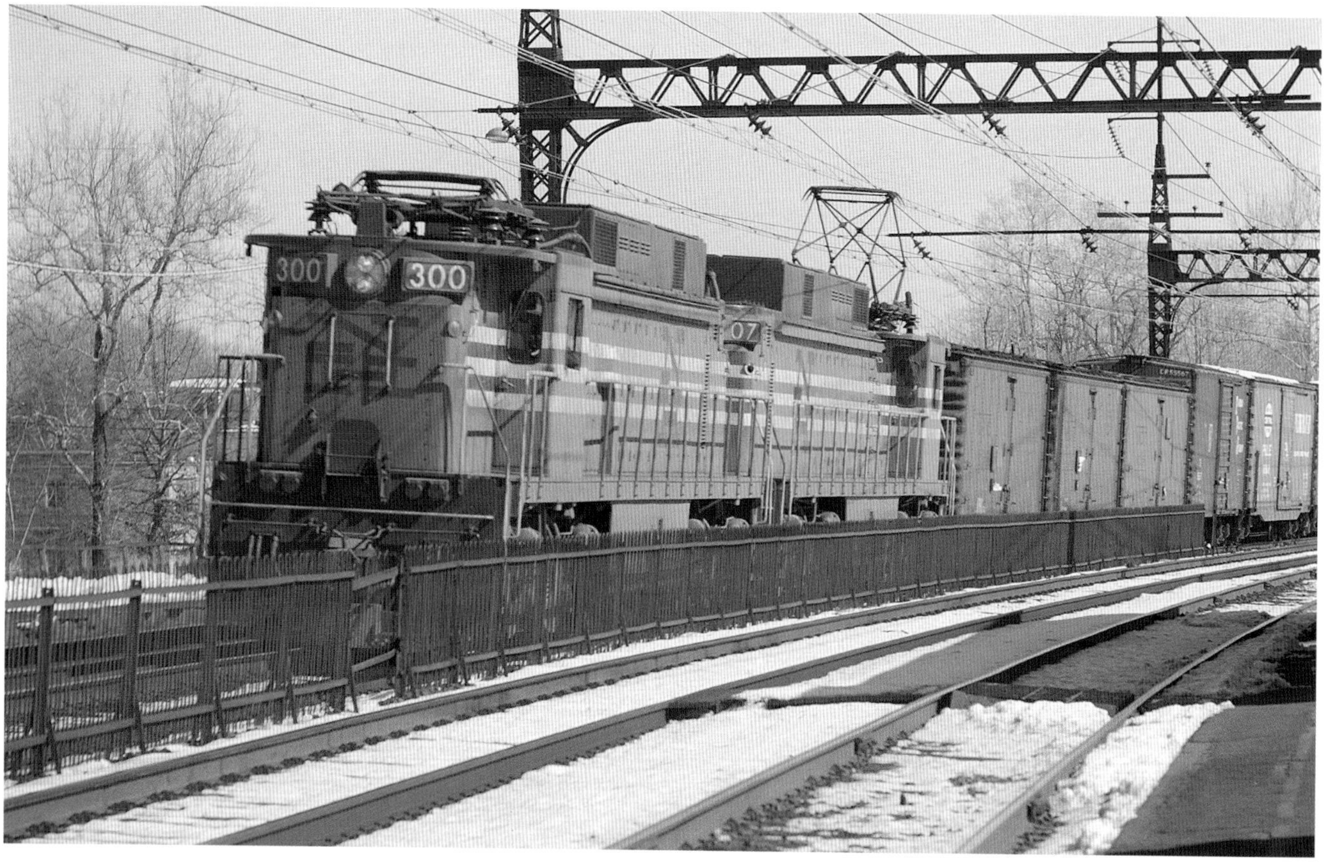
300
300

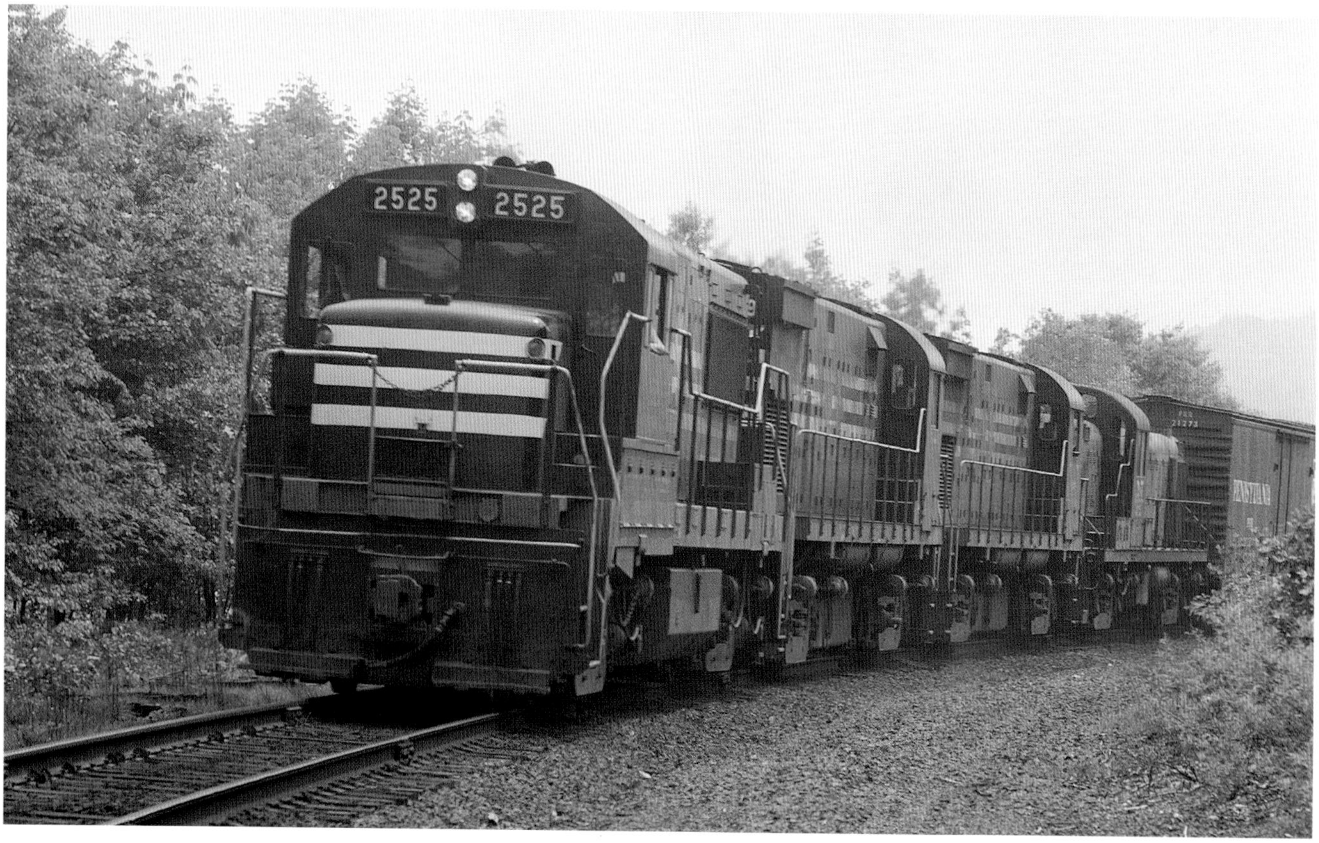
2525
2525

the New Haven's problems. A driving force would be the new Penn Central's plans for routing freight, which would seriously cut the New Haven's revenue share by rerouting traffic via the B&A interchanges, thus "short-hauling" the New Haven. After several years of Pennsylvania-New York Central opposition, the Interstate Commerce Commission ruled that the Penn Central was required to take over both the New Haven's freight and passenger operations as a condition of merger. It was ironic that the Pennsylvania, which had sought to control the New Haven for more than 30 years, vigorously opposed such a move in the 1960s. On January 1, 1969, the New York, New Haven & Hartford Railroad lost its identity, becoming two divisions of Penn Central.

Above: Proud until the end. Train No. 26, the *Merchants Limited*, heads into New Haven Station on its way to Boston in July 1968, six months before the New Haven's absorption into the Penn Central. This 15-car train still looked handsome despite the New Haven's many difficulties. *Peter McLachlan*

Opposite, top: Two Virginian electrics led by the 300 haul a Cedar Hill-Bay Ridge train west through Milford in 1966. Two of these units could easily haul any train of 125 cars, the New Haven's limit on the mainline. *Thomas J. McNamara*

Opposite, bottom: U25B No. 2525 and two others, along with an RS-3, deadheading to Danbury for local service head through Indian Wells State Park, west of Shelton, Connecticut, on the way to Maybrook in 1967. The 2525, built in Erie in November 1965, was the last locomotive built for the New Haven. *Thomas J. McNamara*

155

EPILOGUE
Aftermath

At the time of the Penn Central takeover, a number of difficulties beset New Haven passenger service. On the West End, the older multiple-unit cars were aged and plagued with breakdowns. Numerous failures on the catenary system, especially the 60-year-old triangular catenary west of Stamford, caused frequent delays. The Penn Central received Interstate Commerce Commission (ICC) permission to cut New York-Boston and Springfield service in half, in part because of the loss of most of the U.S. Mail traffic. The remaining Boston trains were diverted to Penn Station, and were hauled by PRR GG-1s west of New Haven and by E-8s east of that city. Most Springfield trains connected to Shore Line trains in New Haven, and many FL-9s were transferred to Brewster to operate former New York Central commuter service through to Grand Central without changing to electrics in North White Plains.

This stone-arch bridge in Kent Falls, Connecticut, shows the substantial construction on the Berkshire as it is crossed by a Housatonic Railroad freight in 1994. *Peter McLachlan*

In 1971 Amtrak was formed and took over the Boston and Springfield services and eliminated the New London–Worcester and the remaining weekend Danbury–Pittsfield RDC trips. Gradually, new equipment came and track improvements were made, but mostly on the Shore Line. By 1999 the Amtrak installation of catenary between New Haven and Boston was complete so that trains could run through New Haven without changing locomotives. By early 2002, nine roundtrip Acela Expresses, Amtrak's new high-speed trains, were operating between Boston and New York in 3 hours and 28 minutes. These, along with the regular trains that took 30 to 45 minutes longer, were recapturing a much larger share of this dense market. It took until 2002 to restore the service to the quality New Haven passengers regularly expected in the early-1950s.

On the West End, commuter service, under the sponsorship of New York and Connecticut, began to see improvement in the early-1970s. New multiple-unit cars were purchased and high-level platforms were installed at every station. The two states, together with Metro North, which took over the service from Conrail in 1983, have made steady improvements to the equipment, track, signals, catenary, stations and bridges. Ridership grows steadily every year and the New Haven Line is the single busiest commuter line in the country, hauling more than 100,000 passengers every weekday. It also has heavy weekend and off-peak passenger use and a large business between local stations, especially to Stamford with its numerous large corporate facilities. Beginning in 1990, the state of Connecticut added commuter service, known as Shore Line East, from New Haven to Old Saybrook and New London, with several morning and evening trips.

In Boston commuter service passed from Penn Central to Conrail to Boston & Maine, and then to Amtrak. Several improvements have since been made by the "T" or MBTA. The line from Readville to South Station, along with the Needham Branch, was completely rebuilt in the 1980s, while trains ran over the Midland route (the Dorchester Branch). Massachusetts purchased a considerable amount of new equipment, greatly expanded station parking, increased service and restored it to Providence, and extended it beyond Franklin to a station on I-495 at Forge Park. In 1997, after a 38-year shutdown, two Old Colony lines were reopened to Plymouth and Middleborough (Lakeville). These two new lines, as well as the other routes, have experienced great annual growth and have once again made South Station extremely busy. Plans are currently underway to restore service to Greenbush, Fall River, and New Bedford.

Freight changes have also been dramatic. The early days of the Penn Central were difficult because of an extremely severe winter in early 1969, system-wide congestion that lasted for several years, and the increasingly deteriorated condition of the New Haven's plant and equipment. Naturally, Penn Central wanted the long haul from Chicago, St. Louis, and Cincinnati gateways, and handled traffic to Selkirk to be sorted and forwarded on the former New York Central's B&A line, rather than via Bay Ridge or Maybrook. In addition, the economy of Southern New England changed drastically, with most traditional large industries replaced by high-tech and service industries. This greatly reduced the need for the movement of goods by rail. In addition, low catenaries and bridges along the Shore Line could not accommodate many of the new larger freight cars.

Starting in 1973, former New Haven freight operations began to be split up, and some were discontinued. That same year in a lease dispute with Penn Central, the Providence & Worcester took back its mainline along with some freight branches around Providence. Then, in 1974, a fire damaged the Poughkeepsie Bridge and no more trains ever crossed it. The Maybrook Line east of Hopewell Junction, New York, continued to be used for a daily Selkirk-Cedar Hill train because Penn Central had connected it to the Hudson Line by upgrading the ex-New Haven Railroad Beacon Branch.

In 1976 Penn Central passed to Conrail, which also had great financial difficulty in its early years. In the 1980s and 1990s Conrail spun off a number of lines: the northern portion of the Berkshire and the Waterbury area to Boston & Maine; the Norwich Branch and the Shore Line freight operations in Rhode Island and Connecticut to Providence & Worcester; the lines around Westfield and Holyoke to Pioneer Valley; some Old Colony lines to Bay Colony; the Maybrook and most of the Berkshire Line to Housatonic; and the Hartford Line freight operations to Connecticut Southern. When Conrail was split between CSX and Norfolk Southern (NS) in 1999 the balance of New Haven freight operations went to CSX. This consisted of Oak Point Yard, the New Haven line to Cedar Hill, and some of the lines in eastern Massachusetts around Readville and on the Old Colony. The New Haven mainlines now see mostly passenger trains and local freights. No more heavy-tonnage through-freight trains run on the New Haven except for some Providence & Worcester (P&W) stone trains. In addition, a few freight cars are switched daily in Cedar Hill and Hartford. Once-important New Haven freightyards in Providence, South Boston, New London, Danbury, East Bridgeport, Maybrook, Derby, and Waterbury no longer switch freight cars. Ironically, most of the New Haven freight system that took so much money and effort to consolidate is once again split up among a number of regional carriers like the Providence & Worcester, Housatonic, Naugatuck, Central New England, Connecticut Southern, Bay Colony, and Pioneer Valley. Also ironic is the fact that the first four bear the names of New Haven predecessors.

What of the New Haven in the twenty-first century? It is transporting more passengers than ever into New York City and Boston and it once again is broken up into many entities—just as it was in 1880.